LIVING WITH
QUILTS

FIFTY GREAT AMERICAN QUILTS

✶

PHYLLIS GEORGE

Text by Ann E. Berman

Photographs by Rob Gray

✶

GT PUBLISHING · NEW YORK

Published in 1998 by GT Publishing Corporation
16 East 40th Street
New York, NY 10016

Library of Congress Catalog-in-Publication Data
George, Phyllis.
        Living with quilts / Phyllis George : photographs by
    Rob Gray : text by Ann E. Berman.
            p.   cm.
        Includes index.
        ISBN 1-57719-3555
        1. Quilting—United States—History. 2. Quilts—
    United States—History.   I. Title.
    TT835.G46   1998   98-20387
    745.46'0973—dc21   CIP

Printed in Singapore

10 9 8 7 6 5 4 3 2 1

First Printing

Text by Ann E. Berman
Design by Susi Oberhelman

CONSULTANT: SHELLY ZEGART

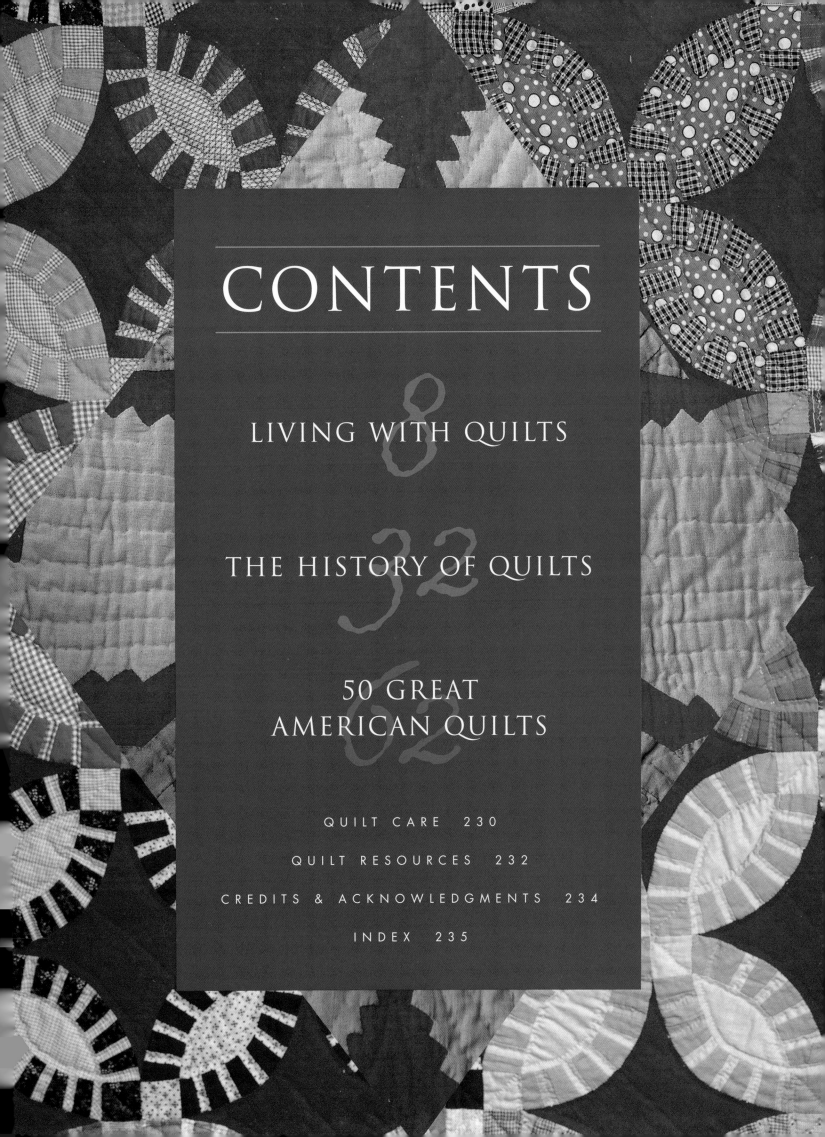

CONTENTS

LIVING WITH
QUILTS

I CAN'T REMEMBER A TIME WHEN QUILTS were not part of my life. From my growing-up years in Denton, Texas, through my years as Miss America, a TV sportscaster and broadcast personality, and as the First Lady of Kentucky, to my current role as a businesswoman and champion of American craft, I have admired American quilts, used them in every place I've lived, and learned a lot about them—and from them. Quilts have very definite personalities: They can be amusing, serious, or romantic. They are also great storytellers, with fascinating tales to tell us about America, about the history of women in this country, and about the people who collect them. Looking at my own collection of wonderful quilts, I can see every chapter of my life reflected in them—each quilt reminds me of a special time or precious memory. I have also discovered that quilts are among the unsung heroes of American decorating. They add warmth and life to any interior, go with any decor. With a little imagination, the dazzling patterns and extraordinary workmanship can transform the entire look and feel of a room.

The idea of decorating with quilts would have come as a surprise to Grandmother George back in Denton, Texas. Like so many of our forefathers (and mothers) Grandmother made quilts strictly for warmth. Some of my earliest memories are of the seductive, colorful piles of fabric she

This Feathered Star quilt from the 1930s adds just the right touch to my patriotic table setting on the front lawn at Cave Hill.

always kept to work with. Mother made a lot of my elementary school clothes, and I wonder if some scraps of those wools and cottons found their way into Grandmother's quilt bags. I remember that her big, round quilting frame was so large that she kept it suspended from the ceiling and dropped it down whenever she wanted to continue her quilting.

Although Grandmother's quilts weren't fancy, I treasured them. My quilts came with me when, fresh from the Miss America runway in Atlantic City, I moved to New York City in the 1970s to begin my TV career. It was an exciting time of life but a little hectic, and when I was exhausted from traveling or feeling under the weather, I'd always cover up with one of those quilts. It was very comforting. Sadly, in my little apartment there was no place to display my quilts, but I always hoped that someday I would live in a country home with space for quilts everywhere. My dream soon came true.

I became the First Lady of Kentucky in 1979. What a wonderful job for a quilt lover! I quickly discovered that quilts are a vital part of Kentucky's heritage—they were everywhere I looked. People there soon learned of my interest and were glad to share their quilts with me. When we were campaigning, many a grandmotherly type would pull me aside and whisper, "I have a trunk just full of old family quilts. Would you like to see them?" Of course I always said yes, and the quilts revealed to me were often absolute heirlooms. I also started to purchase quilts to decorate my new home, an imposing, white-columned Federal style mansion called Cave Hill built in 1821. Collecting quilts became one of my passions, and as I got to know the craftspeople in my adopted state, the promotion of Kentucky quilts and other handcrafted items became my mission.

My son, Lincoln, has always had quilts on his bed. Even as a baby he loved this crib quilt. It was a perfect match for his cradle, handmade of Kentucky cherry.

As I traveled around Kentucky these craftspeople also became my friends. I loved to hear their stories—how the secrets of their craft had been passed down from their grandparents and parents to their own generation. These people were so inspiring to me. They had managed to rise

above the pressures of the fast-paced society we all live in so that they could do what they wanted—what they felt was important—day after day, year after year. It used to bother me when I'd walk up Madison Avenue in New York City and see quilts from Hong Kong, Tahiti, and Taiwan in shop windows. Didn't people know that great quilts were being made right here at home—particularly in my own backyard in Kentucky?

Seeing an opportunity to enhance my state's economic development, in 1981 I approached Marvin

ABOVE: *This pastel floral pattern was given to me as a quilt top, and I had it quilted and finished.*
OPPOSITE: *My pink and white Irish Chain quilt always seems to work well outdoors—as a table covering, picnic cloth, or draped over a wooden bench or wicker chair.*

Traub, then the head of the New York department store, Bloomingdale's.
I sent him a simple cross-section of Kentucky crafts and he was dazzled.
The result was "Oh, Kentucky!" a boutique that opened at Bloomingdale's
(stocked with lots of quilts, of course) and sold out of all of its merchan-
dise within two weeks. We then repeated the same process at
Marshall Fields, Bullocks, Neiman Marcus in Beverly Hills—
even Takashimaya in Tokyo.

Besides bringing the mountain to Mohammed, I also
brought Mohammed (and a few influential others) to the
mountain. I invited quiltmakers and other craftspeople to

As a native Texan, I have a particular fondness for Lone Star quilts. Two of my favorites are shown opposite, at Cave Hill, and above, in my New York apartment.

my annual Kentucky Derby garden parties at Cave Hill in the 1980s and many a New York and Los Angeles socialite found herself unexpectedly falling in love with quilts. *Harper's Bazaar* did a photo shoot at Cave Hill in 1990 that featured at least ten quilts laid out on the lawn. It was a gorgeous photo! During the same years I helped to found the Kentucky Art & Craft Foundation for the development, promotion, and marketing of Kentucky craft. The Foundation opened the Kentucky Art & Craft Gallery on Main Street in Louisville—a Madison Avenue-type boutique in which everything for sale was made right there in Kentucky. Stocked with wonderful contemporary quilts and other crafts, it is still thriving and has become a magnet for Kentuckians, as well as a major tourist attraction for the state.

My enthusiasm for quilts has also been contagious in my own family. My son, Lincoln, eighteen, and his sister, Pamela, fourteen, have grown up with quilts and are attached to their favorites. I have started a tradition of giving Pamela a quilt every Christmas. She looks forward to each new addition and now has quite a few, including the two that hang in her New York bedroom— a Lone Star quilt and a fabulous contemporary quilt called *Memories of Oz*. My New York apartment is brimming with other quilts as well. Those draped over the back of the couch add color and life to the living room, while all of our beds are made cozier by the colorful quilts folded at the foot of each bed.

At Cave Hill every room has a quilt in it. An 1854 Sampler quilt hangs on the wall in the Great Room and has more visual impact than any painting could have in that particular space. It rivets the attention of everyone who sees it. Each square was made by a different woman. The sophistication and intricacy of its design is unbelievable. In the breakfast room, a contemporary quilt by Donna Sharp, done in a Log Cabin pattern of deep blues and burgundies, fills a whole wall and really warms up the room. My Heirloom Basket quilt, made of 3,000 different pieces, is one of the first things guests see, hanging in the two-story front stairwell.

Memories of Oz, by contemporary quilt artist Gladys Boalt, hangs in my daughter, Pamela's, bedroom in New York.

I am constantly thinking of new ways to use my quilts. I remember the spectacular effect we produced at one of the Derby parties by hanging our quilts, one after another, on the white plank fence that stretches along the drive leading to Cave Hill. As the guests were driven to the door in vintage buggies, they passed twenty colorful quilts hanging beneath 150-year-old trees, against blue grass pastureland. What a sight! I have also used my quilts as table covers when entertaining outside in the garden. We placed a different quilt on each table, then protected them from spills by covering them with specially cut glass.

I have found that there are still some people who think quilts belong on a bed—period. True, that was their original function and they look beautiful there, but they can also be used in so many other satisfying ways. For example, instead of putting the quilt on the bed, you could display it folded over a quilt stand or a brass rod attached with decorative brackets to a bedroom door. As you become more comfortable with using quilts to enhance your home, you'll find that they can mix with anything while adding a distinctive element to it. Simply stack some folded quilts on top of a chest or on the shelves of a glass-fronted cabinet, and you'll see how they immediately inject a splash of color to that area of the room.

A great quilt can not only transform a room, it can become a decorative focal point for it. I remember seeing a wonderful antique American quilt in a very posh flat in London's Eaton Square. It was draped over a table set at the end of a sofa and was clearly the source of the beautiful rose and green color scheme in the room. Hanging a quilt like a wall tapestry is also a good way of setting a room's color theme. A smaller quilt, such as a crib quilt or a doll's quilt, can be framed over a wall-hung light box so that the colors of the design shine out like pieces of stained glass. Still another approach is to start with a neutral room palette and

This exquisite 1854 Sampler quilt hangs in the Great Room at Cave Hill. It was one of the first quilts I bought when I began collecting. FOLLOWING PAGES: *Created in the 1860s, this New York Beauty quilt has been showcased at the Museum of American Folk Art in New York City, and is one of the finest in my collection.*

rotate several quilt wall hangings on a season basis choosing, say, a red and green patterned quilt at Christmastime and a pastel one for spring. This way, you can enjoy a variety of color changes throughout the year and get to display a series of old favorites from your quilt collection that usually languish in storage.

Needless to say, any handmade quilt, whether contemporary or antique, should always be treated with care, and you certainly wouldn't want to cut up a quilt or use it in a way that exposes it to staining or fading. But sometimes you may come across remnants of quilts—quilt tops without backing, single quilt design blocks, or a quilt that's been partially damaged. If so, then such otherwise unusable pieces can be salvaged as pillow shams, seat covers, and table runners, or used to upholster the headboard of a bed. Individual quilt blocks can be made into throw pillows or framed behind glass and hung as works of folk art. Quilt tops (unless you want to use them for a finished quilt) can be lined with lightweight cotton fabric and used as curtains, drapes, or window shades, or hung between thin curtain rods as backing for the open panels of a standing floor screen. If a salvaged piece is large enough, you might even transform it into a piece of clothing like a jacket, vest, or long hostess skirt. Several years ago I had a favorite old quilt that was partially damaged made into a pair of charming stuffed bears for my daughter (see page 28). It takes confidence to use quilts in new and unusual ways, but when you start to learn a little about quilts and all of the work that goes into them, that confidence will come naturally. The easiest way to begin enjoying and using quilts in your home is to just shop around and choose what you like.

I'm still learning about quilts. In fact, I have gone through many phases in my collecting. A look through my quilt closet tells my whole history as a collector—from my crib quilts to my traditional patterns, to my 1930s quilts, all the stages I have been through. Lately I have found myself drawn to thematic quilts. I like Lone Stars (for my home state,

The graphic strength of this Sunshine and Shadow pattern complements the brocade sofa and mixes effectively with the Irish Chain quilt on the bed.

of course) and patriotic themes in red, white, and blue. I also enjoy many contemporary quilts like my *Mother of Exile* quilt by Rebecca Siegal, shown below. It makes such a powerful statement about the important women who have influenced the history of our country. Contemporary quilts are doubly impressive to me: I am moved by the people who do this skilled, highly focused work and overwhelmed by the beauty of what they produce.

Every one of my quilts—new and old—has another affect on me as well. Quilts bring me a sense of peace and calm. When I find myself particularly stressed or overextended, a glance at, or snuggling up in, one of

my quilts will always bring me down to earth again, giving me a sense of rootedness—in my country, my family, my own history. I feel very fortunate to have had the opportunity to travel around and meet kings and queens and movie stars, presidents and first ladies—but my quilts bring it all back home. They keep me centered.

Quilts help me to maintain balance in my

OPPOSITE: *Quilt artist Rebecca Siegal made her* Mother of Exile *quilt in 1986 to commemorate the centennial of the Statue of Liberty. It depicts six women who shaped American history: Anne Hutchinson, Betsy Ross, Harriet Tubman, Susan B. Anthony, Emma Lazarus, and Eleanor Roosevelt.* ABOVE: *This red, white, and blue quilt dates back to the Civil War.*

life. Today women have lots of options and I have taken advantage of many of these in the course of my career. While embarking upon these professional endeavors I have also always strived to make my home a warm, nurturing place for my family and myself. My quilts are a big part of that. I want my home to be a retreat—a haven of domesticity—and having quilts around makes my family feel secure and happy. I often think that once a quilt is completed it can't be changed, but our lives are always works-in-progress. We need a little of everything quilted into them to make them whole—a balance of color and pattern to make something truly beautiful.

I have only to look at my quilts to see where I have been—which is one of the best ways to know where I'm going. There's the Crazy Quilt made up of all of the different fabrics we chose when I restored the Governor's Mansion in 1983, and a quilt made up of tobacco silks that evokes Kentucky at the turn of the century. I have quilts that represent good times—romantic times—when I got dreamy over something or someone, and quilts I call my "recreation quilts"—the ones we took with us for picnics at my children's schools and for soccer and baseball games.

Quilts with old fashioned patterns like my Maypole quilt remind me of growing up in Denton, as do my Lone Stars. My crib quilts bring back many happy memories of my children, my Amish quilts remind me of my craft-collecting trips, while my Paper Doll quilt sums up my whole life story—all of the chapters until now. This one-of-a-kind quilt was also made by Rebecca Siegal, and in it I am represented in the yellow swimsuit which I wore in the Miss America competition, and surrounded by miniature, exact replicas of other memorable outfits (like my cheerleading uniform, my Miss America gown, and my red Derby Day suit and hat). Because Rebecca knows I collect antique silver frames, each of these ensembles is presented in a silver frame of quilted cloth. Each outfit is attached to the quilt with Velcro so that I can change the outfit on the image of me in the center of the quilt whenever I want.

This pieced and embroidered quilt from 1890 features rich satins and velvets in an original design.

Many of my quilts have stories. The heirloom Basket quilt that now hangs at Cave Hill is the one that "almost got away." I first saw it in a shop on Main Street in Berea, Kentucky, and I admired it more and more each time I went back. But whenever I asked if it was for sale the answer was always "not for sale." One day it disappeared! I was relieved to find out that it was on a national tour—not sold. When it was returned to its usual place, I felt my old friend had returned and that all was right with the world again. During the holidays in 1996 I was still in my robe with my hair in curlers getting ready for my American Craft Christmas show, when my assistant, Dee

ABOVE: *This charming 1930s appliquéd crib quilt depicting a Maypole dance is one of Pamela's favorites.* OPPOSITE: *Rebecca Siegal's unique Paper Doll quilt shows all the memorable chapters of my life—as Miss America, First Lady of Kentucky, CBS sportscaster and, my favorite role, mom.*

Emmerson, came in to say that my dear friends at the QVC Television Network had brought me a thank-you gift for my work promoting American craft on the channel. I opened the box and there it was . . . the Heirloom Basket quilt! The people at QVC had asked Dee what I would like and she remembered how often I had admired that quilt. When the owner understood how much I loved it, he had finally agreed to sell. He knew his masterpiece was going to someone who would appreciate it as much as he did.

I appreciate all my quilts and can't imagine living without them. In fact, I consider myself a quilt lover rather than a collector, because my quilts are so much a part of my everyday life. I have, and use, a wide variety— museum quality, contemporary, traditional, thematic, crib quilts, and of course my old favorites. I'm very glad to share my collection with you and to show you some fifty other wonderful American quilts in homes across the country. You'll see that from Colonial to cutting-edge contemporary, every interior can be warmer, more welcoming, and more beautifully decorated with the addition of a great American quilt. ☆

The one that "almost got away," this 1935 Kentucky Heirloom Basket quilt is made of 3,000 different pieces. It was the perfect decorative wall hanging for the imposing front hallway at Cave Hill.

PHYLLIS GEORGE , 1998

THE HISTORY OF
QUILTS

A MERICAN QUILTS ARE AS FASCINATING AS they are beautiful. A window onto the unsung lives of their nineteenth-century female makers and an archive of American textile history, they are also a cornucopia of dazzling, imaginative pattern—as graphically compelling as a great painting. Quilts are almost magical in their ability to simultaneously transform the look of any room, keep a sleeping body warm at night, and evoke feelings of comfort and protection. Not surprisingly, a whopping 15.5 million Americans are involved with quilts and quiltmaking. They are a dedicated army that haunts quilt shops, buys tens of thousands of quilt-related books, attends the dozens of museum exhibitions devoted to quilts, throngs Houston's annual International Quilt Festival and Market, and pushes prices for the best historical examples well into the six-figure range.

Small wonder. Every time a quilt is unfolded the viewer experiences a unique double-whammy—a jolt of pure, visual beauty immediately followed by a powerful sense of the individual who created it. For quilts are inescapably personal objects. Intimacy is built into their role—the bedcover under which people were born, made love, tucked in their children, lay ill, and died. Few quilters actually sign their names to their works but they leave their mark in

An old library ladder makes a perfect display vehicle for a collection of vintage quilts, including a Tumbling Blocks, a Log Cabin, and a Baltimore Album. Part of the magic of decorating with quilts is that any group of patterns looks wonderful together.

other ways. Even in a sea of repetitive patterns, no two quilts are the same. The hand and spirit of the maker always wriggles to the surface—in the unusual detail, the odd choice of color—and shows itself to us like a flag waving on a distant hill. We long to cross the divide of time and question this person who, often without benefit of exposure to other good design, chose such arresting colors and arranged them in such a startlingly effective pattern. Where did her ideas come from? Where did she learn to sew? Did she work on the quilt at night? Did she love her husband?

With the soft folds of her quilt in our hands we feel that such answers are almost within our reach, for nineteenth- and early twentieth-century American women poured their souls into their quilting. "My whole life is in that quilt," wrote quilt expert Marguerite Ickis, quoting her great-grandmother, "my hopes and fears, my joys and sorrows, my loves and hates. I tremble sometimes when I remember what that quilt knows about me." Patterns suffused with love, grief, friendship, and patriotism abound; more complicated human themes—rebellion, competitiveness, dry humor, superstition, pride— are played out in their execution. We know all this because we can "read" these objects with confidence. Their makers were our great-grandmothers and their neighbors—not "artists" set apart from the common horde whom we must struggle to understand. We can easily imagine what they must have felt about their quilted masterpieces—the only spot of color in a drab cabin, the only way to hint about the creative fire inside. Even the process is familiar: We understand the ways of needles and thread and can picture ourselves bringing a quilt into being—with unavoidable slowness, with children underfoot and a pot boiling over on the stove.

The process is cozily familiar but also symbolic of some very big ideas: American ideals of patience, small-town ingenuity, thrift, and coop- eration are personified by quiltmakers—women who, night after night, bent over unfinished blocks by firelight, or who gathered chattering around a quilting frame. What they produced is also quintessentially American. Like so

many other examples of this country's folk art, a quilt's beauty and functionality are inextricably linked, with a simple, utilitarian structure that provides almost unlimited design possibilities. Colors and textures can be arranged in thousands of patterns on the "quilt top" then connected to other layers with almost as many kinds of decorative quilting. Every possible aesthetic can be evoked: A trompe l'oeil pattern like Tumbling Blocks confuses and pleases the eye with the same stark geometry as a Vasarely painting, while Victorian Crazy Quilts of silk and velvet lavished with embroidered chrysanthemums and lilies of the valley evoke a landslide in an elegant Victorian closet. Amish quilts stun with simplicity, while the red, white, and green

A Victorian lady poses with a selection of completed patches of a Crazy Quilt. Sewing, embroidery and, of course, quiltmaking, were considered an integral part of the education of any well-bred young girl.

pictorial appliqué of album quilts distill all of the charm of nineteenth-century American folk art onto a single patterned plane.

The quilt has become one of a handful of truly American art forms but the process itself did not originate in America. Quilting is an ancient technique, predating written history. The term comes from the Latin word *culcita*, meaning "stuffed sack" or "mattress," and the technique is known to have been used by ancient civilizations in China, Turkey, and Egypt. The quilt as we know it, however, originated in sixteenth-century England. There, printed cotton fabrics from the Indian port of Calicut (where the fabric name "calico" originated) were imported and used along with chintz to form decorative bedcovers of embroidered or appliquéd fabrics. Whole cloth quilts were common (one large piece quilted to other layers), while others featured a central medallion and border cut out of one fabric and appliquéd onto another. The image of a flowering tree, for example, appearing again and again on an expanse of chintz, might be cut out and appliquéd onto a quilt, becoming the central motif in a new design. This technique became known as "broderie perse," probably because of a perceived resemblance to Persian embroidery.

The American colonists were European in outlook and were proud of their bedclothes (one judged a family's wealth by the richness and variety of its quilts and hangings). They imported or copied European-style medallion quilts using the limited stock of fabrics available. Homemade "linsey-woolsey," a coarse woven fabric, was often used for backing. As the eighteenth-century wore on, the British ban on the American manufacture of fabric continued to make material scarce and expensive and ultimately contributed to the resentments that sparked the American Revolution. As the political climate heated up, patriotic Colonists became determined not to import any more English fabric. Every existing scrap became precious, and complicated appliqué became almost impossible to achieve. Quilts made of recycled bits and pieces became

The illusory qualities of the Tumbling Blocks pattern have made it a favorite among generations of quilters. Here, printed calicoes alternate with their solid sisters, changing the pattern from cascading "blocks" to undulating "ribbons" in the blink of an eye.

more common. It was the beginning of the era of the pieced quilt—a quilting style which would metamorphose, in the early nineteeth-century, into the block-style quilt—pieced block by individual block and then sewn together. It was a style that suited the young Republic exactly, for in this kind of quiltmaking no one block was more important than any other and all were needed to form a strong, unified whole.

In a pieced, block-style quilt, the quilt top is often divided into equal squares (four, or nine, or more). The blocks, each made up of small pieces, are sewn together to create an allover pattern with no central focal point. Each block might repeat a single complete motif or contribute part of one quilt-wide pattern. This technique proved vastly more convenient to the lifestyles of early American women because it obviated the need for a large, permanent quilting frame, so impractical for use in tiny frontier houses and covered wagons. More significantly, it spawned a new, rather startling artistic freedom. Gone were the decoratively arranged floral effects redolent of eighteenth-century wallpaper and furniture design. The effectiveness of the new patterns depended entirely on the choice and arrangement of contiguous colors and shapes. In escaping the fussy pictorial armiture of the medallion style, nineteenth-century women began to produce something uncannily similar to modern painting which, when viewed up close, individual strokes or pieces seem meaningless, but from a distance they form a new and effective whole. The appliqué technique was also quickly harnessed to the block style; its forms gradually became simple, almost stencil-like distillations of themselves, the better to contribute to the look of the whole.

In order to continue their quilting outside in the sunshine, these Louisiana quilters rested their makeshift quilting frame on two pairs of chairs, as they put the finishing touches on a Diamond in the Square variation chintz quilt.

Although the pieced quilt was ideally suited to the use of leftover fabric, after the lean, patriotic days of the Colonial period, most American women bought new materials with which to make their quilts. They chose carefully, juxtaposing contrasting colors and using stunning patterned fabrics to create an overall effect. The

image of the pieced quilt as a thrifty hodgepodge of cast-off scraps is a myth that has been slow to fade. In the absence of other creative or emotional outlets, quilts were so important to American women that they were prepared to go to great lengths and expense to complete them beautifully. In 1863 a Wisconsin woman rode twenty miles on horseback by herself to obtain a particular calico required to complete her peony appliqué quilt. For wives working alongside their husbands on self-sufficient family farms, quilting was a precious escape from the repetitive drudgery of housework. In *Aunt Jane of Kentucky* by Eliza Clavert Hall, published in 1898, the title character imagines all the dishes she has washed over a lifetime piled up and compares the hours required to dispatch that clattering mountain to the many hours of sewing it took to complete one quilt. It was no contest. Quiltmaking was not only a pleasurable aesthetic experience, unlike bed making or dish washing, but also offered her the chance to make something lasting—a monument that would live on after her death.

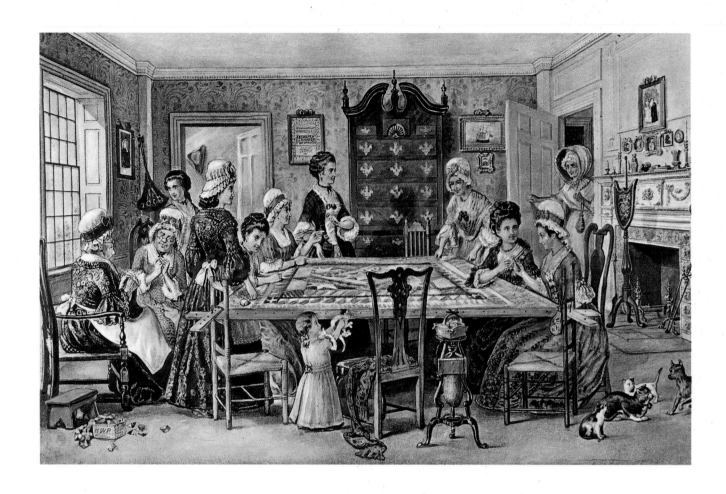

It was also a lifeline to other women. Quilting "bees" (sometimes known as "quiltings" or "quilting parties") at which many women worked on a single quilt, taking turns around the quilting frame and in the kitchen

ABOVE: *Even in a elegant urban setting like this, the nineteenth-century quilting bee was one of the most important ways for women to keep in touch with one another— to gossip, give and receive advice, and exchange quilt patterns. Some of these gatherings might last several days.* OPPOSITE: *A group of Fort Lauderdale, Florida, women work together on a quilt in the Sunbonnet Sue pattern—a simple, evocative design first popularized during the Depression.*

preparing goodies for all, were welcome bright spots in an otherwise lonely rural existence. In more densely populated areas a housewife might attend twenty or thirty such events in a single winter. The quilt became an all-purpose pretext for female social gatherings of all kinds. Quiltings were held to create a momento for a departing friend, provide salable objects for a good cause, or simply to replenish a neighbor's stock of bedcovers. They might last several days. Quilting folklore—charming, but unsubstantiated—tells us that when the quilt was finally finished, all unmarried girls present would catch hold of its edges and a cat would be tossed into the air

from its center. When the flustered feline landed, the girl closest to him would rejoice: She would be next to wed. At a wedding, the "entertainment" would include a display of quilts made by the bride (more than a dozen were often completed by her nuptial year). Girls got started on these showpieces at kindergarten age and soon excelled at making small, even stitches, lest their efforts be dismissed as "toenail catchers."

At all such occasions, new or unusual patterns would be examined with great interest. If a woman saw something she really liked, she would hurry home and make a sample "block" to be filed away for future use. These patterns were not just beautiful; many also expressed meanings plain to their viewers. A tradition of symbolic communication had originated in Europe where needlework had long been used to tell a story to a largely illiterate audience. (If you saw a pineapple, for example, you'd know someone meant to express hospitality). American quilt patterns took up this legacy with mourning quilts (coffins, black borders, and the embroidered names of lost loved ones), marriage quilts (intertwined rings and borders that encircled the quilt without a break), and the friendship or album quilt—a sort of "this is your life" pattern full of symbols pertinent to the maker or recipient. Inspired by the autograph albums and sentimental verses that were all the rage in nineteenth-century America, an album quilt often incorporated the signatures of the makers as well.

Patterns quickly sprouted picturesque or amusing names inspired by bibical references, the trades, nature, love and courtship, buildings, literature, Western migration, and national politics. "Drunkard's Path," "Straight Furrow," and "Delectable Mountain" (after a phrase in John Bunyan's *Pilgrim's Progress*) are examples of these creative monikers. Such names allowed for easy reference in heated quilting discussions—although not if you were newly arrived from another part of the country. Names for the same patterns changed from state to state, and from generation to generation. Not surprisingly, over 4,000 different ones have

The gentle lines of the Double Wedding Ring pattern soften this platted rush bench, making a perfect nest for a beloved collection of vintage toys.

A shift change at a textile mill at Fall River, Massachusetts. The huge demand for new fabrics ensured that the mills were kept busy.

been identified. Their origins are almost entirely unknown but were likely inspired by whatever creative quilters saw around then—unusual flowers, the setting sun, a pattern of shadows at twilight. Once in circulation, patterns would be handed down from mother to daughter, exchanged at quilting bees and state fairs, carried west in covered wagons, or disseminated by itinerant peddlers anxious to sell the specific fabrics they required.

Particularly in the growing urban centers, there was an increasing number of such fabrics from which to choose. By 1836 the U.S. had become a world power in cotton production and processing. The cotton came up from the South and was processed in New England. During these mid-century decades, each year 120 million yards of calico came out of mill towns like Manchester, Vermont, and Lowell and Chicopee, Massachusetts. The American market, ravenous for anything fresh and fashionable, consumed a large percentage. One thousand new fabric designs were created annually, beautifully colored with natural, and later, bright, colorfast chemical dyes. Young girls, eager for gainful employment and a bit of fun, willingly left their farms to become "mill girls," only to end up working long hours in crowded conditions at incessantly whirring machinery. Young men also left their rural homes for the factories and shops of a rapidly growing, urban, industrialized America.

These changes spelled the beginning of a new social order that came to be known as "The Cult of Domesticity." By the 1840s the family farm had ceased to be the main unit of production. Men went out to work each day while the women stayed at home to raise the children. The home was declared the woman's official and only sphere and it was deemed her sacred responsibility. The outside world was seen as dangerous, encroaching, morally suspect. Every wife and mother was charged with creating a soothing, protected, spiritually uplifting precinct from which her family

By the turn of the century, the American textile industry had been going strong for sixty years, although now its mostly female labor force came from the immigrant population rather than the American farm.

could safely operate. Books and advice columns in magazines and newspapers were rife with cheerful suggestions, trumpeting the importance of the decorative environment to the cause, and lest any woman have second thoughts about the whole thing, counseling the necessity of "keeping busy."

Quilting suited "The Cult" in every particular: It was an act of nurturing, an aid to home decoration and a worthy, time-consuming occupation. It was also the perfect handcraft for a new technological age. Other types of home production, including spinning and weaving, were quickly being rendered obsolete by industrialization, but quilting fed upon it. The first mass-marketed sewing machine and the invention of permanent aniline (chemical) dye—both in 1856—brought quilters new levels of convenience and variety. Fabric choice skyrocketed and by 1860, 130,000 sewing machines had been sold. The advent of the railroad put everything—

ABOVE AND OPPOSITE: The mass marketing of the Singer sewing machine in the 1850s pushed quilting to near-mania proportions by mid-century.

Scientific American.

THE ADVOCATE OF INDUSTRY, AND JOURNAL OF SCIENTIFIC, MECHANICAL AND OTHER IMPROVEMENTS.

VOLUME VII.]   NEW-YORK, NOVEMBER 1, 1851.   [NUMBER 7.

THE
Scientific American,
CIRCULATION 16,000.
PUBLISHED WEEKLY
At 128 Fulton street, N. Y., (Sun Buildings,)
BY MUNN & COMPANY.

Hotchkiss & Co., Boston.
Dexter & Bro., New York City.
Stokes & Bro., Philadelphia.
Jno. Thomson, Cincinnati, O.
Cooke & LeCount, San Francisco, Cal.
Courtenay & Wienges. Charleston, S. C.
John Carruthers, Savannah, Ga.
M. Boullemet, Mobile, Ala.
Barlow, Payne & Praken, London.
M. M. Gardissal & Co., Paris.
Responsible Agents may also be found in all the principal cities and towns in the United States.
Terms.—$2 a-year—$1 in advance and the remainder in 6 months.

RAIL-ROAD NEWS.

Railroads in Europe.

We have rather been consoling ourselves with the idea that our recent railroad enterprise was greater than that of all other nations together. This seems to be a mistake, for the Continent of Europe, mixed up with despotic governments, appears to be as truly alive to the importance of railroad communication, as the most go ahead of all our States. The London Times has recently been publishing statistics of the progress of the different countries, which exhibit these results:—Belgium has 532 miles of railways, 353 of which have been constructed and worked by the State, the remainder by different private companies. The expense of constructing the whole has been £9,576,000, or £18,000 per mile. The annual expenses are 63 per cent. of the receipts, and the profits three and a half per cent. on the capital. In France there are 1,818 miles of railway under traffic, 1,178 miles in progress, and 577 miles projected. The cost of construction per mile has been £26,832, and the whole expenditure requisite for the completion of the 3,573 miles is estimated at £95,870,735. The average annual net profit on the capital employed does not exceed two and seven-tenths per cent.

In Germany there are 5,342 miles of railway in actual operation, 700 in progress, and 2,414 miles projected. Of the railways in operation, 1,842 miles were within the Prussian territories, and 771 miles in the Dutch Netherlands, the Danish Duchies, and the ex-German Austrian provinces, and therefore only 4,571 miles can be considered as strictly within the Germanic confederation. Two-fifths of these 4,571 miles were constructed and worked by the State, the remainder by private companies. Those in Prussia, however, are all the result of private enterprise. The expense of construction of the 5,342 miles is estimated at £12,500 per mile, being single track only. The working expenses are about fifty per cent. of the receipts, and the net profits are nearly three per cent. In Russia a railway from Warsaw to Cracow, 168 miles in length, is in operation; one connecting Warsaw with St. Petersburg, 683 miles in length; and one of about 400 miles, from St. Petersburg to Moscow, is in progress. A railway for goods from the Wolga to the Don, 105 miles in length, is also contemplated. In Southern Russia a line of railway between Kief and Odessa has been surveyed. In Italy no extensive system of railway has yet been executed. A few lines, diverging from the principal cities, such as Naples, Milan, Venice, Leghorn, and Florence, are alone in operation. In the kingdoms of Sardinia, Spain, and Portugal, railways are only in prospective.

By multiplying £1 by $4,85 we can arrive at the cost per mile of some of these roads. It will be observed that the French lines—the highest—cost $130,135,20 per mile, or nearly three times as much as those of Massachusetts, the cost of which averages $43,781.00, or about £9,000. If the European lines pay at such an enormous cost, need we be afraid?

SINGER'S SEWING MACHINE.---Fig. 1.

Figure 2.

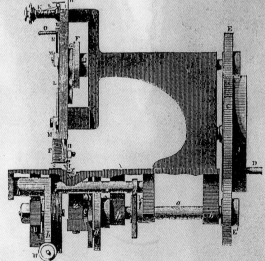

The accompanying engravings represent a perspective view, figure 1, and a side elevation, figure 2, of Isaac M. Singer's Sewing Machine, which was patented on the 12th of last August. A is the frame, made of cast-iron, and B is a cast-iron standard to support part of the working machinery. C is a large driving wheel, worked by the handle, D. E is a small second wheel, driven by C, and works the shaft that vibrates the needle; E' is another wheel to work the shuttle shaft, a, hung in the bearing straps, b b, fig. 2. F is a round plate on the revolving shaft of E; it has a small roller stud on its inner face fitting into a plate, G, slotted of a heart-shape, to answer the purpose of a cam. This plate, G, is secured to the vibrating arm, H, to which the needle, I, is fastened. The needle performs three strokes up and down during one revolution of the large wheel, C. The thread, J, of the needle is supplied by a bobbin, K, and goes through an eye in the needle, near its point. The cloth is laid flat on the table on the top of a small rough-faced roller S, with the edge to be sewn under the needle. The cloth is held down by a pad, R, acted upon by a coiled spring, P;

this pad is raised by a pin, O, and kept fixed by a catch bar, N, which presses against a shoulder piece, M. There is another shoulder piece, M, to secure the arm, L, of the pad, R in its place. When the cloth is laid on the table, on the wheel, S, the catch, N, is thrown out, and the pad, R, is pressed on the cloth by the spring, P, and is retained firmly in its place but still allowed to be carried forward as it is stitched. The way in which the stitch is performed is by two threads, one supplied with a shuttle, X, the other by the needle, I. With-

out two threads, no good stitch has yet been made by any sewing machine. X is the shuttle carrying a thread which passes from a pirn inside through a small eye on the side next the needle. Now, to form the stitch, which is just like the lock or link of a chain, the thread in the needle, after having passed through the cloth, opens, and the shuttle passes through this loop, therefore, when the needle is drawn back, and the shuttle also to the end of its raceway, the two threads are drawn tight, forming a link drawn on the cloth, and thus link after link of these threads form the seam. The drawing of the threads tight, and the forming of the loop on the end of the needle for the shuttle is an essential feature to the successful working of these sewing machines. For this purpose the shuttle, X, has a motion to coincide with that of the needle, I, and it is imparted by the same devices, d, fig. 2, being like plate, F, and Y like cam G, only the shuttle runs horizontally at right angles to the needle; e, fig. 2, is the shuttle arm, and Z is the guide or raceway, in which it runs. Thus the motions of the needle and shuttle are explained. The other lettered devices not explained are those belonging to the cloth-feeding motion. The roller, S, that moves the cloth has a rough face, and rotates, but moves round slowly, only making its movements forward the length of a stitch for every stitch taken; this is done by catches or pallets, a well known way to do so. These pallets are vibrated by a rocking shaft, f, having a bar, g, on it, which is moved by a cam, c, on the shaft, a. To the small rocking shaft, f, there is secured a suspended lever, h, having a collar, h surrounding said shaft, near its bearing end, i. This lever has a hook, V, on its lower end, to which is affixed a setting screw, W. The hook, V, catches on the hand of an arm, T, which has pallets or catches in a box, that catch into notches on the shaft of the feed wheel, S; every time, therefore, the lever, h, is vibrated, the feed wheel, S, moves the cloth the exact length of a stitch forward; the set screw, W, is for regulating the length of feeding the cloth forward to make short or long stitches.

This machine does good work. The patent claim will be found on page 390, Vol. 6, Sci. Am. The agent of this machine is W. H. Shepard, No. 256 Broadway this city.

Things to be Invented.

Among the things that are wanted by every body is a substitute for pen and ink. It seems that a single instrument ought to perform the function, and that fluid ink may be dispensed with. Cannot some substance be found, simple or compound, that will make an indelible mark upon paper, being hard enough also to hold a fine point? Or cannot paper be so prepared, without great addition of expense, as to aid the purpose?

THE CHRISTIAN HAT.—The improvements of the age have reached almost every thing except the abominable flower-pot hat, that so much needs the kindly attention of reformers. We are glad to notice that attention is being directed by some of our public journals to the unreasonableness of a stiff and perspiration-proof covering for the head. The flower-pot hat cannot pretend to beauty; it is certainly uncomfortable and unhealthy. Why then shall we not seek a substitute? The hat should be very light and porous, and by all means soft or elastic; and if any article of our dress calls for especial ornament, the covering of the head speaks most loudly for something to set off the front that slightly distinguishes one man from another. The Turban is probably most susceptible of such modifications as would be most easily adjusted to the purposes required; and we think some such change of the head-dress would require little urgency to get into general favor.

The Sanitary Commission collected thousands of quilts for the Union soldiers during the Civil War. RIGHT: *Bazaars were held during the war years to raise money for the Sanitary Commission.*

machine and fabric—within easy reach. Not surprisingly, by mid-century quilting had reached near-mania proportions. In a family of three daughters one could easily expect a production of forty quilts, and some women made several hundred over a lifetime.

There were also new reasons to make quilts. The dawn of the nineteenth century saw the rise of the "benevolent society"—female-fueled, often church-related organizations that toiled on behalf of the poor and carried out missionary work. Reform movements like the abolitionists also picked up steam. All of these causes needed to fund their good works, and quilts proved to be dependable money makers at bazaars and church sales. With a "signature quilt" it was even possible to raise money twice-over by charging for the right to place one's signature on the quilt, and then selling the finished product. (Lesser positions along the sides might cost ten cents, while those in the middle would cost five times as much.) In the 1860s, well-heeled citizens would sometimes buy a quilt at a Civil War fund-raising event, only to turn around and offer it again for the Cause. The Sanitary Commission, a private organization assisting the War Department and Medical Bureau in providing for the comfort of the men at the front, became the single largest consumer of quilts, in 1863 collecting 5,459 of them for distribution in Hartford, Connecticut alone. In the blockaded South, fabric was too scarce for quilting to flourish, but in the North it continued apace, now featuring patterns with names like "Underground Railroad."

Another popular new pattern was "Rocky Road to Kansas." Between 1840 and 1880 more than 500,000 Americans made the one-way journey west, leaving everyone they had ever known behind, jolting along in uncomfortable wagons, bravely forging ahead into unknown territory. The pioneer woman's all-purpose psychological and practical solution to the miseries of her transient life was her cherished cache of quilts. On the journey they lined wagons, wrapped

Emigrants such as this family moving to Nebraska in the 1880s would have found their quilts invaluable on the hard journey west.

breakables, padded hard wooden seats, and even served as makeshift coffins when, as happened with unnerving frequency, a family member expired along the way. Louisa Frizzell echoed the sentiments of all women on the trails when she lamented to her diary: "I feel tired and weary. O the luxury of a house, a house!" Once a woman had attained the nirvana of a rough-hewn log cabin or damp sod hut, quilts took on other duties—covering doors and windows, forming impromptu furniture draped over benches, establishing a vestige of domestic cheer, and adding warmth to bedsteads. They also paved the way to other women. Newly arrived pioneers immediately sought out fellow quilters for life-sustaining sessions of quilting lore and pattern exchange.

By this time many patterns were also being disseminated by mail—introduced in the pages of national magazines like *Godey's Lady's Book* and *American Agriculturalist*. Popular traditional designs were familiar to women from coast to

Godey's Lady's Book was the fashion and homemaking bible of the nineteenth-century American woman. Both its pages and those of American Agriculturalist *were important sources of new ideas for quiltmakers.*

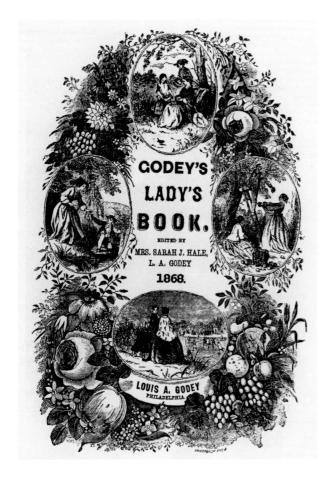

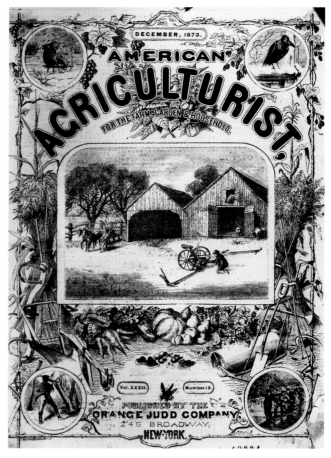

coast. Then in 1876 when the Centennial Exhibition opened its doors in Philadelphia, the impact of exposure to international style pushed some quilters in quite a different direction. Strolling through the vast exhibition

halls in Fairmont Park, ten million visitors stared wonderingly at displays of Japanese porcelain and lacquerwork—not to mention an inspiring exhibition organized by Britain's Royal School of Needlework. The result was the Crazy Quilt. This pieced conglomeration of asymmetrical shapes made out of rich fabrics like silk, satin, and velvet was united with a web of elaborate embroidery. The name, which suits its jumbled style, actually came from its resemblance to the "cracquelure" or "crazing" on a porcelain vase. These busy, luxurious beauties were soon sweeping Victorian America.

The Centennial also focused new attention on the old patterns. One hundred years into America's history, and with the Centennial celebrating the country's beginnings, anything "Colonial" was suddenly back in style and the patchwork quilt was considered the quintessential example of this nostalgic period. The Centennial was also America's introduction to the English "Aesthetic Movement" which, by preaching decorative unity, encouraged the production of still more "fancywork" and glorified home decoration. The exhibition also spotlighted American workmanship and design and provided American women with the chance to examine an unprecedented selection of each other's quilts. State fairs and quilting bees were one thing, but the scale of the quilt exhibition at the Centennial did much to complete a national picture of what might have, until this point, seemed an insignificant, local craft. Women from Nebraska to Alabama could suddenly see that quilting was beautiful, important, and common to them all—that it was the art that patched them all together.

The years that followed (1875-1900) were a golden age of American quilting. All of the groundwork had been laid—hundreds of patterns developed, the sewing machine invented (with a quilting attachment by 1892), fabric choice broadened—and as if that weren't enough, the complex construction of late-nineteenth-century women's fashions created plenty of waste fabric that could be handily recycled into quilt production. It was the age of the elevator and the telephone, but for women this galloping new technology spelled little change in focus. The decoration and protection of the family domicile continued to be their primary interest, and quilt production continued automatically and prolifically. As late as 1889, Lucy Larcom noted in *A New England Girlhood* ". . . we learned to sew patchwork at school . . . almost every girl, large or small, had a bed-quilt of her own begun with an eye to future house furnishing."

As the new century got underway, however, quiltmaking became increasingly commerical. Eager to promote the sale of material, thread, and related goods, big city department stores sponsored quilt contests and lured

customers with quilting novelties. One catalogue adver-
tised "the prettiest, queerest, most grotesque, scariest and
original patterns." Printed patterns were beginning to
replace the oral tradition of dissemination. While some
historians mourn the disappearance of creative quilting

The elaborate displays of Oriental objects on view in the main building of the 1876 Philadelphia Centennial Exhibition thrilled American visitors and influenced the output of a generation of quiltmakers.

during this period, others point out that important new genres of quilt design

were still appearing, including the distinctive quilts being made by the Amish in

Pennsylvania and elsewhere and the unique appliqué quilt that was developing

in Hawaii. Back in the East, some quilts moved entirely out of the domestic

sphere to become proud banners for social and political causes. Temperance

Unions were fighting hard for prohibition, the abolition of child labor, and the

institution of the eight-hour work day. Turn-of-the-century quilt patterns

reflected these concerns and the quilts themselves continued to play their

familiar role at fund-raising events.

With the start of the First World War, the need for fund-raising

escalated. The coffers of the Red Cross and other nursing societies required

constant replenishing, and homemakers were urged to create "Liberty Quilts"

During the quilting revival of the 1930s, quilt patterns reflected America's interest in popular culture. This Cartoon quilt, made in Los Angeles in 1934, is typical of those made during the Depression.

for home use—saving storebought blankets for our boys overseas. After the war, patterns continued to reflect popular concerns—like the flight of "Lucky Lindy" in 1927. The distinctive silhouette of his famous airplane became the basis of an oft-used quilt design. Cultural icons like Mickey Mouse also appeared as quilting patterns, now printed in popular columns in newspapers like the *Kansas City Star* and disseminated by self-interested corporations like Stearns and Foster, a batting company. In the spirit of flagpole sitting and phone booth stuffing, quilters bid for their "fifteen minutes" of fame, producing "record-breaking" quilts made up of tens of thousands of tiny pieces. Competition heated up and by the 1930s Albert Small of Ottawa, Illinois, had topped many other contenders by making a quilt containing a whopping 63,467 hexagons. (Although quiltmakers were overwhelmingly female, this competitive, high-profile project was apparently unusually appealing to the other sex.)

Mr. Small's feat reflected renewed public interest in cheap entertainment. The Great Depression had come to America. But like so many developments in our history, that sad experience was actually a boon to quiltmaking. Under the auspices of the WPA, quilting was taught to unemployed women, while the Index of American Design recorded thousands of examples of the American decorative arts, preserving a body of quilt design that would otherwise have been lost forever. When in 1933 and 1934 Chicago's Century of Progress Exhibition featured a quilt contest sponsored by Sears Roebuck and Company, the $1,200 prize attracted over 25,000 entries. It was ultimately presented to Margaret Rogers Caden of Lexington, Kentucky, for her fabulous "Feathered Star." Other contemporary patterns sported streamlined Art Deco designs, but many featured comforting, sentimental themes, in patterns like "Sunbonnet Sue" and "Grandma's Flower Garden." Colors ran to the pastel and quilts were as pretty and unthreatening as the floaty dance frocks of Ginger Rogers.

The mid-century years were lean ones for American quiltmaking. The process had become homogenized by "labor saving" pre-cut quilt kits, and many women who had entered the workforce during WWII wished to remain there. Quilting seemed dated—even a trifle provincial. But just as interest in quiltmaking began to slow, appreciation of its past glories began to grow—rapidly. In 1924, the opening of the American wing at New York's Metropolitan Museum of Art conferred new status on American arts and crafts and other institutions soon followed suit. The quilt found itself transformed from the product of a homey hobby to a respected historical object. Historical and art museums around the country mounted exhibitions of antique quilts and began to purchase important examples for their permanent collections. The counter-culture of the 1960s focused new attention on the creative self and embraced the quilt for its handcrafted naturalness. Art was changing quickly, and as Rembrandt was succeeded by Rauschenberg on American museum walls, the graphic power of the quilt was suddenly seen in a new light. In 1965, an exhibition at The Newark Museum, "Optical Quilts," was the first to treat the quilt as a work of art—not a craft—on a visual par with the Op Art of the era.

The real breakthrough year for quilt afficionados everywhere was 1971. An exhibition organized by Jonathan Holstein and Gail van der Hoof entitled "Abstract Design in American Quilts" was held at New York's Whitney Museum of American Art. Holstein and van der Hoof purposely hung a stunning selection of graphically patterned quilts against stark white walls—far from the homey period rooms that had been their usual exhibition venues—and in their catalogue essay, compared them favorably with great works of abstract art. Quilting itself—indeed craft of any kind—was de-emphasized in favor of the power of overall design. The show was a revelation to the American public and the art historical establishment alike. Art critic Hilton Kramer of the *New York Times* wrote: "For a century or more preceding the self-conscious invention of pictorial abstraction. . .the anonymous quilt-makers of the American provinces created a remarkable succession of visual masterpieces that anticpated many of the forms that were later prized for their originality and courage."

Quilts were suddenly hot and private collecting now began in earnest. Quilt hunters went foraging in the countryside in search of masterpieces they hoped could still be recovered from attics and cellars. Often they were rewarded. Some gravitated to Lancaster County, Pennsylvania, and other Amish strongholds looking for the dark, geometric, wool quilts made there. Others searched the hills of Kentucky or the shady streets of small Midwestern towns for traditional pieced and appliquéd quilts of every description. Many important examples were saved from neglect or destruction as the great quilt collections of the late twentieth century began to take shape. New collectors were aided by a series of comprehensive new quilt histories that identified hundreds of patterns and placed them in a useful historical perspective. New quilt dealers opened their doors, and auction houses began to offer quilts in their Americana sales. Inevitably, prices for the best examples began to rise steeply.

Quilt scholarship also improved greatly, aided by surveys like The Kentucky Quilt Project. In 1981, in response to statewide advertisements by the project's organizers, Kentuckians brought their family quilts to designated locations to be examined and recorded. In this way over one thousand such quilts were documented and the Project became a model for similar operations in other states. In turn, the treaures they unearthed became the focus of a new kind of history. Conventional historical study had long devalued the role of women—they left few written records and took little part in politics. But under the influence of the women's movement, quilts were being recognized as important historical documents illuminating the unwritten history of

The 1971 show at the Whitney Museum in New York City, "Abstract Design in American Quilts," showcased quilts like this 1900 Amish example, revealing an uncanny similarity between these quilts and the great abstract paintings of the twentieth century.

nineteenth-century American women, shedding new light not only upon the craft of quilting but upon the lives of the quilters themselves.

The past few decades have been a new "golden age" for America's quilters. By last count, over seven million Americans are involved in quilt-making—creating a profusion of styles and using new materials that would have surprised and fascinated their ancestors. Some quilters continue to use traditional techniques and patterns, while others graft modern imagery onto the traditional template of piecework or appliqué. Their quilts continue to be used as decorative bedcovers, to celebrate important events, and pro-claim support of contemporary causes. The AIDS quilt project has attracted thousands of participants and thousands of quilts were also made to mark our nation's bicentennial.

But these familiar genres have been joined by a late-twentieth-century addition—the art or studio quilt. Such a quilt is not meant to be used as a bed-cover, but to be hung on the wall like other fine works of art. In abandoning the design and construction requirements of a functional quilt, contemporary quilt artists have freed themselves—just as early block quilters once did—from the strictures and expectations of the old ways. Although many studio quilters start with traditional methods, including piecing or appliqué, they may go on to incorporate material from other visual artistic disciplines like collage, photography, and printmaking. The conventional rectangle may be stretched or reshaped. No subject matter—emotional, political, or confessional—is off limits. The quilt medium has been recon-figured as a blank canvas to be manipulated and bent to the will of the artist to express his or her artistic vision. Titles are evocative and expressive and pieces are often accompanied by an artist's statement of intent.

Because of art quilting's enduring relationship to "craft," its practitioners enjoy a freedom denied other visual artists—and access to a wider audience. Unusual or difficult aspects of their art seem far less threatening than

The AIDS quilt, containing more than 20,000 panels honoring people who have died of the disease, is displayed in Washington, D.C.

those that characterize works by cutting-edge painters and sculptors. As Robert Shaw wrote in *Quilts: A Living Tradition,* "Thousands of Americans have slept preacefuly under wild and powerful abstractions they would probabaly never even consider hanging on the walls of their home." This same connection, however, has also proved frustratingly limiting. Quilt artists are constantly wrestling with questions like, "Where is the boundary between craft and art?" and "Why is one less important than the other?" Some artists find identification as a "craftsperson" limiting, both artistically and financially, and have ceased to refer to their productions as "quilts," preferring the term "fabric collage."

Fortunately, along with the new genre has come the establishment of venues in which quilts may be properly shown and appreciated. Quilt National, a juried show held in Ohio every other year since 1979, was founded by quilter Nancy Crow to promote contemporary quilting as an art form. The exhibition attracts thousands of entrants and helps set the standard of excellence for the field. Houston's annual International Quilt Festival and Market serves as a vast gallery for art quilters as well as a handy one-stop shopping venue for prospective purchasers. Among these are curators of corporate collections who find the art quilt the perfect antidote to the white starkness of many corporate settings. Dozens of other shows held around the country at commercial galleries and small museums, along with the large number of symposia, lectures, and conferences planned every year on the subject of art quilting, illustrate the depth of interest in this new field.

Visitors to these shows are surprised, then charmed, by the sight of quilts hung with the same reverence and importance as paintings or prints. Many are surprised to discover that quilts need not be confined to "country" settings filled with rustic pine furniture and samplers. Decoratively and aesthetically, the American quilt is now being recognized as among the most versatile—and affordable—of art objects. Quilts add color and softness to all horizontal venues from the bed to the tabletop—then leap effortlessly onto vertical planes as striking wall hangings. Stark white rooms come to life with the addition of

bright color and graphic design, while the charming clutter of Victoriana craves the addition of a quilt's clean, precise patterning. When you add the extraordinary output of contemporary quilters, there is simply no decor—from French Provincial to Southwestern—that cannot be completed beautifully with a quilt. Drape it, fold it, hang it, enjoy it. It's a little piece of American history, a smart investment, and a timeless piece of design. "Patchwork? Ah, no!" says the nineteenth-century heroine of *Aunt Jane of Kentucky*. "It was memory, imagination, history, biography, joy, sorrow, philosophy, religion, romance, realism, life, love and death." It is an American quilt. ✩

An exhibition of American quilts at London's Commonwealth Institute in the 1970s celebrated the quilt as an international art object.

So rich and varied is the American quilting tradition that it would have been impossible to include examples of every genre and date. Instead, this selection features fifty great American quilts dating from the early years of the nineteenth century to the present. Each is different from its fellow, each is beautiful and an excellent example of its kind.

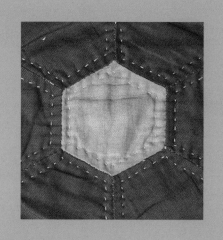

Here are quilts of every stripe—Crazy quilts and Amish quilts, Depression quilts and Album quilts—a satisfying sampling of

RICAN QUILTS

the endless wealth of pattern, color, and historical interest that characterizes this art form. Every example has been allowed to tell

its own fascinating story and to-gether these stories make up a larger saga—that of the America in which the quilts were made.

Each of the choices is presented in a different setting, demonstrating the amazing versatility that makes quilts so at home in every American home. Beauty, function, history, decorative clout —the American quilt has it all.

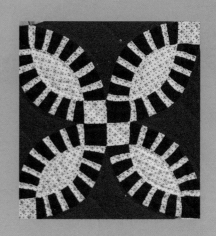

THE VICTORIAN CRAZY QUILT

"OF ALL THE CRAZES which have engulfed some of us there is none which has taken a deeper hold on the fair women of our land than this one of crazy patchwork," wrote the editor of *Dorcus* magazine in 1884. Strong talk but old news. By 1884 the fad for making Crazy Quilts had already been going strong for eight years—ever since the Centennial Exhibition in Philadelphia, in fact. In 1876 millions of fascinated Americans had thronged the exposition's Japanese Pavillion to see displays of porcelain, lacquerwork, embroidered silks, and screens—all featuring the asymmetrical, irregular Asian aesthetic. In a nearby pavillion, an exhibition of fancy embroideries by the Royal School of Art Needlework was also proving quite inspiring. The result: A new type of quilt composed of irregularly shaped pieces of velvet, satin, and silk (often beaded or embroidered with Victorian motifs) connected with a complicated web of intricate embroidery. As its patterning was thought to resemble the crazing on a porcelain vase, the new style quickly became known as the Crazy Quilt.

In retrospect, the appearance of the Crazy seems almost inevitable. Its rise coincided with the American discovery of the Aesthetic Movement—an English-born decorative cult that preached the importance of handwork and of the "aesthetic interior" (When Oscar Wilde, one of the movement's more famous champions, toured the U.S. with a sunflower or lily in his lapel, those symbols of High Aestheticism popped up on Crazy Quilts every-where.) American decorating guru Charles Eastlake urged women to create "artistic homes" for their fami-lies—with layers of pattern and design like those supplied by the Crazy Quilt.

By the 1870s fabric was available in bewildering profusion, including a newly increased supply of im-ported and domestic silks, and the complicated women's fashions of the day were producing a ready supply of sumptuous scraps. The Crazy concept was also a natural outgrowth of the album or friendship quilts of an earlier day into which makers had incorporated precious snip-pets of wedding or christening dresses, and upon which they had embroidered cryptic symbols known only to themselves. Construction-wise, makers of Crazy Quilts simply borrowed from the system already required by the traditionally geometric Log Cabin pattern, cover-ing a foundation square of muslin or calico with their chosen pat-tern of scraps and stitching them into place.

Set against a black and white tiled floor, the velvety, embroi-dered randomness of this Victorian Crazy Quilt seems as precisely patterned as an Oriental rug.

At all levels of society Crazies became quite the "thing to do." The very genteel New York School of the Decorative Arts, an important arbiter of taste, declared the silken, heavily embroi-dered, Asian-influenced Crazies to be the height of fashion—the more needlework in evidence the better. Because of their appearance, Crazies were sometimes referred to as Japanese silks or embroidered quilts, although very few were actually quilted. Most were technically quilt tops, single layer, parlor conversation pieces, not bedcovers—to be displayed over the piano, the sofa back, or covering an ottoman. For the reverse side, women often used recycled silk dresses. One dress might do, as the labor-intensive crazies tended to be quite small.

Makers reveled in the fact that the edges of their mas-terpieces would never be tucked under a mattress, adding many decorative flourishes to finish them. In this exam-ple, silk, velvet, and lace have been combined to form a charming border that emphasizes the fragile materials and rich color scheme of the quilt. Oscar Wilde's sunflower is front and center, as are other traditional Crazy motifs like fans and birds. Because of its construction, a Crazy was naturally organized into squares, but in this one those squares form no unifying design. Each square is an indi-vidual composition; the whole is balanced only by the strategic placement of Japanese-influenced fans. The maker has provided many embroidered motifs to anchor the design but has not overwhelmed her creation with cobwebby white stitching.

With all its flowers, lace, and fans, this is a rather feminine quilt that would not have been out of place in a Victorian boudoir. In fact, it is just the perfect size to drape over a satin chaise longue. Missing are the more masculine elements—commemorative ribbons from military campaigns or horse shows and the other sym-bols of family history that many Crazy Quilts feature. This example seems less about memory than about beauty, richness, charm. We wonder if its maker was pretty. Maybe she was dark with delicate bone structure. But of course, we will never know. ✦

GRANDMA'S
FLOWER GARDEN
QUILT

WE ALL KNOW ABOUT Depression glass and Depression art, but if there were such a thing as a Depression quilt this sunny rendition of Grandma's Flower Garden would be it. It is typical of tens of thousands of similar quilts made during the period. The design was such a ubiquitous choice for 1930s quilters that one Ohio county fair made Grandma's Flower Garden quilts a whole separate prize category. What was the attraction? How did this nice, but rather ordinary-looking hexagonal design manage to become the toast of 1930s America? The answer is that Grandma and her flower garden were just what Americans were looking for during those difficult years.

The pattern was based on an old pattern called Mosaic, or Honeycomb, which had been around for over one hundred years. This old-time familiarity was much in its favor. Since the 1920s, Americans had been living in suburbs full of "Colonial" architecture, buying American furniture, and scouring antique stores for weather vanes and frakturs. The country was in the throes of a "Colonial" revival —a catch-all term signaling a revival in American traditional design. Actually, the tastemakers who spoke from the paper pulpit of popular magazines and newspapers took much of their inspiration from nineteenth- not eigtheenth-century objects. But any way

you defined it, American quilts were perfect exemplars of the "Colonial" movement—representing good old-fashioned American coziness, know-how, and thrift. Homemakers who had inconveniently thrown away "outdated" family quilts now set about making new ones.

They had plenty of encouragement. Bright, clear, colorfast fabrics imported from Germany, banned during WWI, were once again available and the stores were full of modish prints in a rainbow of pastel hues. Because clothes were shorter and skimpier (a 1928 dress required only half the fabric of a 1918 model), companies were looking for other ways to sell dress goods. The homemade quilt, appropriate to the Colonial interior and a low-cost, practical object, was their answer. By now even the most remote farm family had access to newspapers and mail order catalogs, and in them companies pushed paper patterns, ready-cut patches, transfer pattern kits, and stencils. Quilt columns written by "Aunt This" and "Grandma That" blanketed the country, replete with suggestions for "real American" patterns, updated with tempting, fruity color schemes. The lonely farm wife in Iowa enjoyed knowing that she was making the same quilt as her big-city sisters. Nobody minded if the finished products tended to be rather homogenous. Rather like the movies of the day, Depression-era quilts were a form of optimistic, diverting, popular entertainment—"Soft covers for hard times," as one prominent quilting expert has called them.

Grandma's Flower Garden was particularly diverting. It required the quilter's full attention. Every single one of its thousands of hexagonal pieces had to be exactly the right size or, when the quilt was put together, it would never lie flat, pull as one might. Most quilters used a template to assure consistency. Beginning with the central hexagon, rings of hexagons were constructed and then those were put together to form an allover pattern. The design had another advanatage: It could be made from a wide variety of small, leftover scraps and still look wonderful. Pattern companies offered many different varieties, marketed under the names Variegated Hexagons, Garden Walk and The Diamond Field. *The Kansas City Star*, a well-known hotbed of quilting lore, provided a version called Ma Perkins' Flower Garden, named after a character on a popular radio program. No matter what it was

An expanse of pure sunshine, this quilt could light up even the darkest room. It's easy to see why this cheery pattern was especially popular with Depression-era quilters.

called, every one of these quilts promised what makers of this era were looking for—a walk through a happy flower garden, along endless sunny paths.

This quilter has ensured the success of this illusion, using a butter-yellow background and natural flowery colors. Her hexagonal shapes might be flower beds in a formal garden or just one bed of much larger flowers with multi-colored petals. The use of fabrics with floral motifs continues the theme. Unlike some other Flower Garden quilts, this one was clearly made with large amounts of newly purchased fabric—not bits of scrap—and has been carefully planned. Even on the rainiest days, it can't help but lift the spirit. ✪

THE CENTURY OF PROGRESS QUILT

THIS QUILT WAS MADE as an entry for the mother of all quilt contests. In the depths of the Depression—in 1933—Sears Roebuck & Company set out to get maximum bang for its buck. Having erected a snazzy modern pavillion at the Century of Progress, Chicago's Centennial and World's Fair, the company decided to stage a crowd pleasing, highly visible PR event. Recognizing a chance to increase sales of the quilting supplies with which its 1930s catalogues bulged, Sears decided to sponsor a quilt contest. In January 1933 they announced a grand prize of $1000 for the best new quilt made in the United States, to be submitted for examination by their committee by May 15th of that year—just four months later.

As they knew it would, the announcement immediately struck a nerve. The Colonial revival of the 1920s coupled with quilting's appeal as low-cost Depression entertainment had contributed to a mini-quilting boom. The contest also tapped into the American spirit of competitiveness that flourished during this period. Along with the question of how many people could fit into a phone booth and who could sit longest atop a flagpole, Americans wanted to find out exactly who was the maker of the most beautiful American quilt. Many quilters, of course, wanted to be that person. The $1000 in prize money was certainly an incentive—you could buy a new Ford for $490 in those days—but the heady shot of glory the winner could expect was just as appealing.

Twenty-five thousand women answered the call—more contestants than for any other contest before or since. Sears' publicity machine immediately began spewing statistics, crowing that the 25,000 quilts had taken 5,625,000 hours—or 642 years—to make, and that the company had a 12-foot-tall mountain of entries still to examine. Newspapers wrote human interest stories about contestants working night and day, neglecting their cheerful and encouraging families. The field was open to almost anyone. Contestants could use prepared quilting kits or they could make their own patterns. They could submit an existing quilt (although not an antique one). A $200 bonus would be given to the quilt that best commemorated Chicago and the Century of Progress itself. Winners would be selected in stages—local semi-finalists selected at the big-city stores, finalists whose quilts would be shown at the fair, and finally the big winner. Everybody who won got a cash prize.

Made for a quilt contest at the 1933–34 Chicago World's Fair, this quilt is a Deco dream of the Machine Age. Its clean geometry and metallic hues lend a modern touch to any setting.

Thirty finalists were selected, and then finally the grand prize winner—Margaret Rogers Caden of Lexington, Kentucky. The $1000 prize was awarded for her green Star of the Bluegrass quilt, which thrilled the judges with its intricate stuffed work—raised, stuffed patterns filled with string or batting. The quilt was then presented to the nation's First Lady, Eleanor Roosevelt, and has since disappeared. The Star of the Bluegrass was a traditional pattern as were those of the other two top winners, and so skewed was the judge's taste in that direction that the bonus prize for a Century of Progress Commemorative quilt was never even awarded. Ironically, subsequent research has proved that Mrs. Caden's traditional quilt was made in a very modern manner: She supervised the work, but it was actually pieced and quilted by four other expert Kentucky quilters. She did not share the prize money with any of her helpers and, as they were afraid to lose their jobs during the Depression, none of them ever protested this inequity.

Those who had labored long over commemorative Century of Progress quilts did complain, however—rather loudly. Where was the $200 bonus prize? Sears silenced the mob with an exhibition of their quilts during the fair's second season—filling the room with the streamlined, Utopian symbolism that epitomized the fair itself. Sears mysteriously kept no records of the event, but it is likely that this example was among them. Its maker is unknown but even without explanation, its evocation of the highway system and skyscrapers of Chicago is unmistakable. The central cog represents the march of industry while the spokes of the surrounding wheel showcase all of the methods of "modern" transportation of which Chicago was already becoming a hub. The buildings, in sophisticated Art Deco colors, are reflected in Lake Michigan as the stars twinkle above.

Buried in the shadow of the Star of the Bluegrass this quilt had no chance of winning. The judges must have hated it. But to contemporary eyes it is both startlingly modern and wonderfully nostalgic—and, by all means, a winner. ☆

THE
FLYING
GEESE
QUILT

WHY HAS NOBODY EVER traced the cultural history of the United States through the more than four thousand names of its quilt patterns? Political preoccupations could be documented through names like Tippecanoe and Tyler Too, while the young country's concentration on building would be evident in names like Barn Raising and Log Cabin. Nature, courtship, the trades, religion, literature, each has contributed dozens of pattern names. A researcher would only have to look at frequency, regional preferences, and dates of these creative monikers to be able to compile a fascinating history of American society.

Or maybe not. Though the idea is a captivating one, any researcher who attempted such a history would soon realize the problem. Pattern names have always been a moving target—of unknown origin, impossible to date, and prone to change from decade to decade, region to region. Nobody knows why a particular pattern was called Rock Glen in Kentucky or when or how it came to be called Lost Ship on the West Coast. Another pattern, originally called Indian Trail, has gone through at least a dozen other names, including Storm at Sea. It's not really difficult to see why: With just a few changes in scale and angle a familiar pattern will suddenly look different and so be rechristened. Since patterns were frequently recreated from memory, what was Lover's

Knot in Virginia might have been made differently out in Illinois yet have been called by the same name. So while history can be used to study quilts ("This is the Tippecanoe and Tyler Too pattern so this quilt couldn't have been made before 1840"), quilts have trouble returning the favor. That Tippecanoe quilt may have been made in 1920 and have been called by some other name to boot. Cultural historians would have a heck of a time using it to chart interest in nineteenth-century politics.

Yet pattern names have other lessons to teach. Charming and evocative, they are a testament to the bottomless well of creativity of American women—and to their legendary coping skills. There were no eighteenth-century names from which quilters could draw—early diaries and letters are almost devoid of such references. But the country was growing quickly and as more and more designs appeared, women used their eyes and imaginations to create a vital, common language of quiltmaking. Patterns of pieced shapes were seen to resemble everyday objects and became Straight Furrow, Mariner's Compass, and Flat Iron. All human activities were fair game: Drunkard's Path poked fun at the consequences of excess, the fun of square dancing was evoked in Hands All Around. The names trip off the tongue, cheerful and whimsical, reminding us of the great joy quiltmaking was to its practicioners. Although by the late nineteenth century all of that whimsy was standardized—pattern publication had become big business—differences, regional and otherwise, persisted.

Even today this pattern, Flying Geese, is referred to by a whole family of avuncular names. It isn't hard to

A traditional chevron pattern resembling geese in flight gains added punch from the use of subtle combinations and striking, unusual colors.

imagine how they all got their start: Looking up into the early-nineteenth-century sky, women would have seen wild geese winging in formation, abstracted by the height at which they were viewed. Then looking down at a triangular patchwork pattern in use since the Revolution, they would have put two and two together—but no two would have done it exactly the same way. The same pattern became known as Wild Geese in Flight and Wild Goose Chase, while those names and others, like Birds in the Air, were applied to other versions in which the triangles are turned at different angles, used in blocks instead of strips, and so on.

Our example, made in cotton prints in Ohio in about 1900, is a classic. This is the original Flying Geese pattern—dating back to the eighteenth century—in which variously patterned triangles are stacked in strips and alternated with those of a single fabric. (Earlier makers sometimes used toile, or chintz for the latter.) In addition to the intrinsic attractiveness of the pattern, its enduring popularity may have something to do with its inexplicable facility to look the same right side up and upside down. ✩

THE WOOL UTILITY QUILT

"IN THE SUMMER TIME when we put a bed outside to sleep, we used those because they were tough . . . everybody saved the wool scraps until they'd get enough to make a quilt. . . . Nearly everybody just pieced those in long strips no matter how they came…And it was a real big deal if you got a piece of wool that had a bright color to it because they were always monotone—greys and darks."

So wrote Mrs. Loyce Wood Sage of Gallup, New Mexico, of the making of early twentieth-century wool utility quilts—the "forgotten men" of American quilting. These abstract mixtures of leftover wool may lack almost all of the usual attractions of antique quilts—precise patterning, intricate stictching, brilliant color—but they boast a power and an aesthetic freedom that quite makes up for it. This was the realm of "anything goes." Never meant to go to the state fair—or even the back bedroom—these quilts were made when nobody was looking. They could be daring, they could be abstract, they could be anything that interested or pleased their makers.

Although this maker probably thought only of combining wool scraps to produce a warm bedcovering, her quilt has all the aesthetic presence of a great abstract painting.

Also known as hired-hand quilts (because they were often assembled for use by farm workers or employees and often made only large enough to cover a cot), such quilts were usually constructed of leftover suiting material,

sometimes enlivened by scraps of old blankets, sweaters, and the odd bit of upholstery fabric. Even if no large pieces were available, the quilt could be made with fabric snippets too narrow or small to be used in any other way. The quilter cut out a paper template and then sewed each small piece to this foundation, building up the design as she went, relying on the contrast of light and dark fabrics for maximum effect. When each block was finished, she simply ripped away the paper and the "pattern" remained. The blocks could then be sewn together to form the quilt.

In the case of this quilt (made in New York State around 1900), the template must have been the size of the entire quilt. No individual blocks were involved. This complicated, unusual design was put together the way an artist paints a picture—as a cohesive whole—not as a series of connecting pieces. Wherever did she start? There is no clear "middle," no subtle underlying pattern to give us a clue. It is possible that some of the strips were laid on after the quilt top was already completely covered, achieving a layered effect that enhances the final product. Otherwise, what we see is a fiesta of piecing that, for all of its apparent randomness, must have taken hours and hours of the maker's time. The result is an eerily modern, extremely balanced and pleasing composition with more than a nod to Cubism. What thrifty, rural woman who probably never saw the inside of an art museum, turned out this quilt top that looks for all the world like some early twentieth-century painter's evocation of the fall of capitalism, jazz rhythms, or possibly Manhattan at night? We will never know.

These days, when "Outsider Art" is winning increasing numbers of fans, such works are of particular interest. But before utility quilts are canonized by the art establishment, questions remain: Did the maker of this quilt ever intend it to be a work of art of any kind, or was she simply tying to produce something cheap, quick, and warm for outside and other rough usage? Did the freedom from the stars and bars and careful appliqués of her "best" quilts—so carefully judged by country neighbors—lead her to these powerful abstractions, or were they merely the serendipitous result of a hand blindly reaching into the grab bag of scraps? If the former, we would indeed characterize our anonymous quilter as an "Outsider Artist," and if the latter, well, the beauty of utility is the very soul of another cherished American tradition—folk art. Either way, the viewer wins. ☆

THE
LOG
CABIN
QUILT

NOBODY IS QUITE SURE how the Log Cabin pattern came to be—or when. Some experts date its appearance to around 1850 while others insist it didn't show up until the beginning of the Civil War. It might have come originally from our northern neighbors—an 1880s reference calls it Canadian Patchwork—and then again, it might not have. It's a bit of a mystery. Most quilt patterns are anonymous—their origins lost to us—but many people continue to debate the genesis of the Log Cabin pattern because it is one of the most important in all American quilting.

It is also among the most long-lasting. From its beginnings in Victorian America, through the heyday of Amish quiltmaking in the 1920s, through its pre-eminence during the Depression, to its continuing popularity today, the Log Cabin pattern has endeared itself to successive generations of quilters. No pattern is more versatile, and none is more obviously American. The Log Cabin is, well, the log cabin of quilt patterns, effortlessly evoking upright ideals of democracy, nature, community, and honest work. The names of its best-known variations—Courthouse Steps, Dark and Light, Streak of Lightening, Barn Raising, Windmill Blades, Pineapple, Straight Furrow—echo this perception. They are all about building a nation. They take us back to an earlier, and we assume, simpler time.

The pattern's great popularity in the years just after the Civil War was no accident, for it evoked the memory of the martyred president, Abraham Lincoln. His end-lessly mythologized pioneering youth seemed to live again in every quilt top, in which "logs," like the ones he split so often, were carefully "stacked," one above the other. Not only that, but in evoking a shared past—the carving out of the forests of both North and South to settle the new land—the pattern seemed a hopeful vote for the endurance of the Union. This patriotic tradi-tionalism stood in stark contrast to the other popular quilt pattern of the 1880s and 1890s—the Crazy Quilt. The Crazy was influenced by foreign aesthetics and was thoroughly modern. It was unpredictable, luxurious, and progressive. The Log Cabin quilt (although, ironically, made with the same unique process of press-piecing) represented order and simplicity. It was a quilt of equal pieces presented in straightforward lines. It was America incarnate.

But all this would have counted for little if the pattern had not been so visually appealing or so inexhaustible in its variations. These are divided into two types: Patterns like Pineapple and Courthouse Steps are made up of the same block repeated throughout the quilt top. Barn Raising, Straight Furrow, and others are allover patterns in which various blocks are made differently in order to form the pattern. The names are evocative, but also descriptive. Courthouse Steps seems to distill all of the Federal architecture that housed official nineteenth-century America, while Barn Raising seems a bird's-eye view of the rising rafters. All patterns depend on the

A member of one of quiltmaking's most enduring and versatile families of patterns, this quilt is made up of thousands of fabric "logs" arranged so that their pineapple-like shapes appear to over-lay a grid of squares.

juxtaposition of colors and the contrast of dark and light logs to produce their effect and all have the ubiquitous hearth or chimney, at the center of each block. These, like the logs themselves, may also be of any size or color, but in the case of the hearths, that color is traditionally represented elsewhere in the quilt as a unifying element.

This Pineapple Log Cabin quilt was made in 1875 by a member of the Crutchfield Family of Fayette County, Kentucky. It is made of wool challis, hand-pieced and then finished with a hand-cranked sewing machine. In this example the hearths are represented by large, dark blocks surrounded in red. These alternate with blocks in which small logs form smaller and smaller squares within squares until the whole looks like a swiftly turning fan or one of the revolving patterns magicians employ to hypnotize their subjects. The effect is certainly mesmerizing, particularly since the pattern of squares appears to be overlaid with a dark grid of pineapple-shaped objects, running obliquely from corner to corner. What a commotion! The quiltmaker has wisely kept her palette rather monochromatic and not tried to achieve too many effects with light and dark. This quilt gets most of its impact from sheer intricacy. It must have taken months to prepare and put together. ☆

MINIATURE
HEXAGONAL
PATCHWORK
QUILT

"PERHAPS THERE IS NOT patchwork that is prettier or more ingenious than the hexagon or six sided." So enthused America's first fashion magazine, *Godey's Lady's Book,* in 1835. Apparently our quilter agreed, producing this example around 1840. The pattern was still fairly new on these shores, where it was sometimes called English patchwork because of its popularity in England. It had appeared there late in the eighteenth century, appropriately called Mosaic or Honeycomb after its distinctive appearance. Although once considered important in its own right, these days hexagonal patchwork has been relegated to its role as ancestor of one of the twentieth century's mega-patterns, Grandma's Flower Garden. That particular arrangement of hexagonal patches in a series of "flowerbeds" surrounded by "walks" is charming and familiar, but it is interesting occasionally to look beyond its pastel charms to earlier examples of this very beautiful—and difficult—brand of quiltmaking.

Hexagonal patchwork was skilled and tedious work. The pattern's construction called for a series of hexagons made by fitting each smaller hexagonal piece into the angle formed by two others. Every larger hexagon then became its own "patch" as it were, finally being sewn together in impressive numbers to form an entire quilt top. *Godey's* spent many paragraphs instructing potential makers, going into great detail, counseling the use of a template, and warning that "of course the patches must be all exactly of the same size." It was an important caveat: If any single piece was off-kilter, the whole quilt would pull awkwardly, spoiling the effect. *Godey's* assumed that its readers would use calicoes, and recommended punctuating the quilt top's allover design with hexagons of white muslin.

Our quilter seems to have followed these instructions—up to a point. Her quilt is indeed made of various calicoes, which, because they were made in the 1830s or 1940s, are today considered rare and interesting in themselves. Some may have come from England or even from India, although it is difficult to be sure. The United States was already printing millions of yards of calicoes each year and our mills were known for knocking-off popular European patterns. It's also difficult to determine the precise age of an early fabric, as popular patterns were printed and reprinted, year after year. As to the strategic

Hand-tied fringe and subtle, earthy colors give this quilt of honeycomb patchwork a modern, rather sophisticated look, although it was actually made about 1840.

use of white, our maker has put a whole new spin on that. Here off-white hexagons, arranged in lines not clusters, have been used to form an unusual design that must have amazed and impressed her contemporaries.

The typical cluster motif is nowhere to be seen. Instead, the quilt top's design is a single large hexagon that "echoes" from the center to the border, one hexagon surrounding the next. Off-white hexagons visually separate their colored neighbors, keeping everything from becoming too dense. This pattern is similar to that of many early-nineteenth-century quilts that featured a central medallion surrounded by other motifs. Here, all is done with hexagons, but our attention is drawn irresistibly to the center nevertheless. Then there is the unusual scale of the patchwork: One hundred years before competitive quilters won Depression newspaper contests by putting tens of thousands of itty-bitty pieces of patchwork into a single quilt, this maker dazzled her audience with the miniaturization of her forms. Her hexagons are tiny, beautifully sewn, and number in the thousands. When we remember how difficult it was just to get everything cut out and sewn properly, we are suitably impressed.

The colors are idiosyncratic for a quilt of this era. Their sublety, and the preponderance of grayed, beigy, earthy tones is unusual. The strong reds, dark pinks, greens, and indigo blues typical of the period are missing; indeed strong contrast of any sort isn't this maker's style. The result is strangely modern, a carefully blended blond mélange that would not be out of place in a roomful of 1950s Swedish modern furniture. Making this all the more fascinating is the quilt's pale, hand-tied fringe, which, though it might remind us of a twentieth-century bedspread, actually signals something quite different. The presence of such fringe almost always means that the quilt was made before the Civil War. ✩

KATHLEEN SHARP'S QUILT oeuvre is something of a Magical Mystery Tour—an invitation into another dimension of architecturally rich spaces. Stand before *Colonnade* or *Big Top* and, suddenly, we are carried away to another place. The air feels different. "Viewers make of these quilts what they will," says the Bay Area artist of her compelling quilted Neverlands. "I simply engineer space, incorporating both the known and unknown, and afford the viewer an opportunity to enter."

It's a very particular niche—this making of mysterious, three-dimensional fabric worlds—and one Sharp came to gradually. "Nobody grows up thinking they are going to be a quilt artist," she points out. "I had always done art of some kind—for a long time it was my avocation. Then one day I said to myself, 'What have you always wanted to do?' The answer was 'Make a quilt.'" As she was living in Washington D.C. at the time, Sharp took herself off to local quilt expert Elly Sienkiewicz who taught her all the basics. Once equipped, Sharp immediately had many ideas, then realized that she didn't know anyone else who was using the quilt medium to make an artistic statement. "I was kind of on my own. I gave myself one year to succeed on my terms, and fortunately it all worked out."

The uncanny sense of depth produced by Kathleen Sharp's Colonnade *makes it the perfect decoration for a small architectural space.*

Sharp loves the tactile quality of her medium, its plethora of patterns, and, above all, the freedom that comes with doing something relatively new. "Nobody is looking over my shoulder saying, 'You must do it this way,'" she explains. "In this field you are limited only by your imagination." To this open-ended discipline, Sharp brings her lifelong interest in architecture. These haunting fragments, corners, and niches inform much of her work, as do specific elements found in late–Bronze Age art. Sharp has traveled to the Mediterranean basin to study these in situ, incorporating individual images and designs found there into her quilts. These influences are particularly clear in *Colonnade,* in which she invokes the sense of a place that is "civilized but close to nature, in a moderate climate, at some altitude but near water." The spiraling symbols decorating the colonnade are those found in Bronze Age pottery and are symbolic of life.

"I like to make places where things can happen," says Sharp. "I've always been drawn to create theatres." If this quiltmaker had been as comfortable with a hammer as she is with a needle, she believes she might even have been a set designer. In *Big Top*, she has created such a place of theatrical possibility—a mysterious seaside pavilion. With its tentlike proscenium arch, it is a many-textured, rather surreal stage set. Anything might happen here, anything might appear—out of thin air or a magician's top hat, or from the wings where actors engrossed in their own private dramas might be poised, ready to make an entrance. Are we inside or outside? The dark, starry fabric above the proscenium adds to the ambiguous, magical mood of a place beyond conventional time. Down below, a black checked floor seems to recede into the far distance, punctuated, like an Alice in Wonderland chessboard, with bits of a fantastical set.

To make her quilts, Sharp begins with a hunt for the right textiles. During this process her focus is intense—

the spark of one colored thread can fuel her search for fabrics that will make the picture she has in her mind or on her drawing board. She works mostly with cotton and cotton rayons, preferring designer and decorator fabrics for their strength and colorfast qualities, as well as shimmering, transparent silk metals. As these fabrics are discovered and pieces shaped by free cutting and tearing, a transformation occurs. What was once a disparate pile of textiles now evokes place, feeling. In *Colonnade* we're suddenly in limitless, sunny space, bordered only by distant mountains, looking up at a monumental construction—a place where human beings have lived for many centuries.

Technically, the composition is held together with machine appliqué and some piecing, stitched into a whole cloth for a front layer, sometimes enhanced with acrylic paint. Quilt construction is traditional, with polyester batting and in the case of *Colonnade*, an abstract patterned backing. Quilting is done by machine, and is what Sharp calls extremely dense stipple quilting. "In the average four-by-eight-foot quilt I use about two miles of thread." she says. As the quilt takes shape, Sharp pays attention not only to its appearance, but to its feel in the hand and the way it lies against the wall.

Small size and graphic punch make Big Top *by Kathleen Sharp a versatile alternative to a print or painting on this stairway wall.*

Sharp feels she has came to the quilt medium at just the right time. "I'm very lucky," she says. "The field has changed a lot during my career and I now feel that it's more generally understood." Unlike some who argue defensively that quiltmaking is art—not craft—Sharp cheerfully points out that it is both. "I don't know what the debate is all about," she says. "I like the fact that quiltmaking brings art and craft together." ✩

THE
BALTIMORE
ALBUM
QUILT

PICTURE A GREAT AMERICAN QUILT and the image of a Baltimore Album is likely to spring to mind. Although these masterpieces of appliqué were made in only one location—Baltimore, Maryland—and over a very short period of time—1846–1852—they have come to represent the epitome of the quiltmaker's art, even of American folk art itself. With their primary colors and simplified floral designs, Baltimore Album quilts bring to mind the frakturs, samplers, and theorems paintings made by nineteenth-century American folk artists. Their idiosyncratic references to Baltimore monuments, boats, trains, and masonic emblems also make them a quilted microcosm of early urban America.

Although Baltimore quilts are the most famous examples of the genre, album quilts were made in many other locations, beginning about 1840. Taking their name from the autograph albums that were so fashionable during the period, many were the result of a group of women getting together to make a quilt to commemorate a special occasion. As many as thirty or forty quilters might work separately on their individual quilt blocks and then meet to arrange, connect, and quilt them into a balanced overall design that could be presented to an honored recipient. There was much good-natured competition among participants, as they struggled to impress—and surpass—each other with their needlework and design skills.

Each contributor typically signed her block, either in pen or with embroidery stitches. Engagements were common occasions on which to haul out the quilting frame, but births, the retirement of community leaders, and deaths were also frequently marked by the making of an album quilt. Just about this time families began to be separated by the pull of the West, and many a weeping woman, departing for parts unknown in a jolting covered wagon, carried with her a quilt containing precious memories of those whom she was forced to leave behind.

In mid-1840s Baltimore, the presence of two superseamstresses pushed album quiltmaking in another—less communal—direction. Achsah Goodwin Wilkins (1775–1854) and her protégé, Mary Evans Ford (1829–1916), are said to have made, or contributed to, a number of the great album quilts to come out of Baltimore during the peak years of their production. Similarity of design, the level of skill displayed, and the lack of individual signatures point to the production of many quilts by just a few talented hands. No two women, however, could possibly have made so many alone. It would have taken an individual maker a year of forty hour weeks to complete a single quilt. Wilkins is believed to have had a number of black (possibly even slave) girls working under her direction while quilts made by "Mary Evans" were probably made by a group of needlewomen who designed and sold single blocks or even whole quilts.

With their simple, graphic depictions of fruits and flowers, monuments, ships, and trains, Baltimore Album quilts are prized by folk art and quilt collectors alike.

This example, ca. 1850, was signed in ink by one Mary E. Johnson. It is divided into twenty-five blocks, many of which are adorned with a generic appliquéd element like a basket of flowers, a bouquet, or a wreath. Specific Baltimore references include a monument inscribed "Ringold", for Major Samuel Ringold, the Baltimorian and martyred hero of the Mexican War of 1846, and an album inscribed "H. M. Smith"—presumably the person for whom the quilt was made. The background is white, the colors primary, and many different fabrics—printed or plain—have been used to give depth and texture to the various elements. Each square is separated from the others by fine quilting, and the whole is surrounded with a twining, floral vine. All have been arranged for visual balance and maximum effect. Similar elements were used over and over again on other Baltimore Album quilts; it was by way of subtle changes that each quilt became a distinct masterpiece within a predictable genre.

Baltimore Album quilts were produced during the years when that city was the nation's leading seaport and the center of its textile industry. But by 1852 those honors had passed to New York. The small town atmosphere that had fostered competitive quiltmaking and communal sewing projects melted away as technological and societal changes swept the country. But the optimisim and freshness that had characterized the new nation lives on in these spectacular works of art—now available only at a price. Prime examples of Baltimore Album quilts routinely sell for six figures at public sales. ✩

THE CIGAR RIBBON QUILT

THE ANONYMOUS WOMAN who designed this cigar ribbon quilt around 1880 didn't play by the rules. It was the height of the "decorative arts" movement—ushered in by the international displays of porcelain, textiles, and furniture at the 1876 Centennial Exhibition—and magazines of the period were exhorting women to improve their family's life by embellishing their homes with "fancywork." Throwaway items were highly recommended because, as the magazines noted, they were within the financial reach of every woman. The maker of this cigar ribbon quilt may have followed their advice but the result was unlike anything envisioned by those dainty, high-Victorian editors: She took a rather hokey idea and created a timeless, highly geometric work of art.

"Timeless" and "geometric" were hardly the watchwords of the era. Influenced by the asymmetrical patterns and clearly outlined forms introduced by Japanese objects at the Centennial, ladies were taking colorful, throwaway scraps of silk and quilting them in unpredictable, allover patterns that resembled the cracalure or crazing of the glaze on old porcelain. The

Victorian quilters couldn't resist turning the silky, printed ribbons that came with their husbands' favorite stoogies into table mats, ottoman covers, and other parlor conversation pieces.

result was known, quite appropriately, as a Crazy Quilt. The irregularly shaped patches were often united into a pleasing whole with complicated embroidery executed in a contrasting color, further adding to the in-your-face, frenzied decorative quality so beloved by Victorians. Around 1870 many women were discovering that this same cobwebby stitching could be used to unite quilts made of another kind of throwaway—the silk ribbons used to tie together cigars at the point of purchase.

By 1880 cigars had become America's favorite form of tobacco. Workers in the thousands of small cigar factories that dotted the country were paid by the bundle and from the resulting practice of bundling finished cigars came the merchandizing idea of using those handy ribbons to proclaim the brand name. These were stamped at intervals along each ribbon, although some of the fancier manufacturers wove them right into the fabric and even added borders and other decorative effects to catch the eye. There were thousands of brand names, often with foreign or masculine connotations, and every combination of letters and printing styles produced its own visual effect. The ribbons themselves were usually made in orange, yellow, or gold—perhaps to indicate the richness of the tobacco—while a smaller number were made in white, red, or blue. And unlike the crackly bands of printed paper used to circle individual cigars after 1900, fabric cigar ribbons were smooth, permanent, and in their own way, rather attractive.

Such silky, decorative little morsels proved irresistible to the quilters of the era. Because of the long, narrow shape of the ribbons, many women adapted the Log Cabin pattern for their creations, applying the ribbons like logs in a pioneer dwelling, one on top of the other, to form geometric patterns. The central placement of the brand name—stacked up like an endless shopping list of catchy cigar store monikers—continued the linear geometry; color variations could add to the look and elaborate embroidery stitching pulled it all together, adding what the Victorians probably considered to be a much-needed decorative element. Of course the gathering of enough cigar ribbons to make a full bedcover was a daunting task and unless a husband or brother-in-law happened to be in the cigar business, many women contented themselves with pillow covers and throws not unlike this one.

This quilter seems to have decided that it was not necessary to prove that every part of the quilt was indeed constructed of cigar ribbons. Instead, her keen visual sense led her to leave badly needed space between printed names, allowing the decorative quality of the printing to pop out at the viewer. The spiderweb shape she chose—rather like the inside of an opened umbrella—is a subtle, unifying pattern, well served by her monochromatic palette of golden orange. Even her stitching—a plain briar stitch—is executed in the same gold-yellow tones of the ribbons. Finally, she leads our eye to the center where she casually reminds us what this quilt is made of. There, fabric ribbons in muted contrasting colors are fashioned into a pinwheel culminating in an astonishing three-dimensional circle of crochet. The result is a tour de force of design in which the usual focus elements of this type of quilt—the printing fonts and symbols, the bold stitching—are merely elements in a unified whole. How un-Victorian. How like the medium of quilting to inspire such a renegade. ✩

THE OCEAN WAVES QUILT

A SINGLE BLOCK of the pattern Ocean Waves doesn't look like much, but put together a whole quilt's worth and you can almost smell the salt breezes. Suddenly, thousands of tiny triangles have formed an intricate, interconnecting pattern that undulates across the quilt top like an abstract rendering of the sea as seen from an airplane, the white caps rising at intervals into the distance. Of course around 1880, when this quilt was made, nobody had ever seen the sea from such a vantage point, but perhaps from the deck of a great liner or a towering lighthouse the view would have been almost the same. In her 1973 book, *American Patchwork Quilts,* Lenice Bacon spins a romantic scenerio of creative pattern-making, speculating that "a fisherman was compelled to be away for many weeks at a time, leaving his wife with her mind and eyes continually concentrated on the ocean, with the result that she introduced the obvious and graceful wave rhythm in her quilting."

A nice thought, but the truth is that nobody knows where the Ocean Waves pattern originated, or why. It is entirely possible that it came into being on the strength of its unique geometry, only picking up its maritime moniker generations later when somebody noticed the strange overall effect of those groupings of triangles. Some people think the pattern first developed in the British Isles during the first half of the nineteenth century. Most known American examples, like this one, date from the second half of the century. By 1894, when the

pattern was mentioned for the first time in print in the *Ohio Farmer*, various versions were already in common use. It took another thirty-four years before any Ocean Waves variation was offered by that national fount of pattern information, the quilt column in the *Kansas City Star*, and three more years until the popular version we see here (with the blocks turned diagonally) was finally published in the *Rural New Yorker*.

Made with one of quiltmaking's most popular patterns, this example of Ocean Waves is a sophisticated blend of pieced triangles and subtle white-on-white quilting.

One reason for the pattern's popularity was its great versatility. By changing the scale of the triangles, the colors, and the angle at which the squares are set, widely

varying results can be achieved. It can be difficult to recognize that any two quilts were made to the same basic pattern. Making the interior squares darker than the triangles can make them "pop out" and become the focus of the pattern. Emphasizing the four triangles at the nexus of any four squares turns them into an eye-catching pinwheel. When the pattern fills the entire quilt it seems to reach beyond its borders to infinity, just as the ocean stretches as far as the eye can see. In such cases the quilting becomes less of a focus than the piecing—every triangle fitting with the next, which when done perfectly dazzles the eye.

Some versions of Ocean Waves can claim membership in the family of illusionary patterns, which, like Tumbling Blocks, are able to fool the eye into thinking it sees something that isn't there. In this quilt, for example, the center triangle in the interior row of each square seems to poke out into space, beyond the confines of its straight side. Yet each of these lines is actually perfectly even—no poking—and if you look again you can see that the illusion of irregularity has been produced by the color and position of the triangles. The same choices have also heightened another illusion—that of undulation of the entire pattern, which seems to dip and rise on the quilt top. The fact that this quilter miniaturized every triangle in her quilt—to allow the complete pattern to fit into the center of the quilt leaving a generous border—lends a flowing, allover quality to the piecework, making it look even more like moving water. Meanwhile, this maker added to the flow by filling the large border with graceful, vinelike quilted patterns, allowing them to wind their way through a diamond quilted field. The quilt is a tour de force of piecing and quilting and must have required countless hours of concentrated labor. But perhaps by the time it was finished, the fisherman was safe at home. ✩

THE "GIFT OF TONGUES" QUILT

BACK IN 1986, Brooklyn quilt artist Robin Schwalb was lucky enough to experience what so many of us long for—a eureka moment when everything clicked into place and she realized that professionally, she had found what she was looking for. "I had started as a traditional quiltmaker," Schwalb remembers. "Then I met an art quilter and her work, together with other art quilts I had seen in books, began to inspire me. I started making what I'll call 'contained crazy quilts.'" What happened next changed Schwalb's professional life: "Somehow I started to put language into my quilts as decorative symbolism," she recalls, "and suddenly, I knew that this was right, that it was what I had been waiting to do my whole life. Now all of my work revolves around language."

The beauty of the written word has been celebrated for many centuries. Consider the gracefully inked characters of the Japanese manuscript or the Medieval incunabulum with its crabbed Gothic lettering. Robin Schwalb's appreciation of written symbolism is peculiarly her own: In her quilts she manages to showcase the abstract beauty of such symbols while incorporating relevant texts rather like found objects in a collage. Unlike such objects however, language can have its dangers: Aware that the natural, human tendency to decode words detracts from their abstract visual power, Schwalb is careful to obscure their meaning (with cropping, small print, over-quilting, obscure language, etc.), thereby retaining the full decorative power of her text.

Her success is obvious in this example, *The Gift of Tongues*, in which two different quotations from the writer Bruce Chatwin give the quilt its focus. The title quotation is most relevant: "Language—the gift of tongues which Yaweh breathed into the mouth of Adam." Schwalb stenciled and photo-silk-screened the text in various parts of the quilt to surround a central black-and-white image of New York in the 1940s, discovered in Japan (of all places), already printed on fabric. Just below the image, an avalanche of obscure text is seen spilling out of that city of a hundred living languages. Near the top of the quilt, repeating photo-silk-screened images of a building being demolished—caught just at the moment of implosion—symbolize an impact powerful enough to cause such a falling away of civilized speech. A narrow band of color near the top of the quilt stands out in a sea of black, white, and gray that seems to echo the written text that for Schwalb gives the work its meaning. "For me, black and white can be rich and colorful."

A myriad of techniques contribute to that richness, from the photo silk screens of the imploding building to the stenciled text. "If I can't find the right fabric (like the Japanese view of New York) I'm forced to make it myself," she says cheerfully. "Besides, I like the fact that people can't tell which is which. It keeps them guessing." To finish the quilt, Schwalb machine-pieced and hand appliquéd the quilt, then handed it over to a professional quilter. This practical decision clearly makes her a trifle defensive: "I printed the fabric and pieced it," she points out. "All she did was stitch the top, batting, and backing together." Schwalb needn't protest. Her quilter is no different than the fabricators used by great sculptors to formulate their pieces, or those who assist printmakers with the final product.

Of course, Schwalb knows this. She trained as a painter and has studied printmaking as well. Her influences are the greats in her former field—"Matisse, Diebenkorn, Kurt Schwitters, and Rauschenberg—his

The evocative calligraphy used by Robin Schwalb in The Gift of Tongues, *echoes the beauty of the Oriental characters on a nearby screen.*

influence is so pervasive I don't even think about it any more"— but in the end, quiltmaking is her lasting love. "I never really connected with painting," she explains. "I love the problem-solving aspect of quiltmaking; I love the craft, the beautiful fabric." Less appealing is the ongoing problem of public acceptance of the art quilt on its own terms. "You still have to get past the prejudices," Schwalb admits. "Say the Q word and people get all warm and fuzzy and start telling you about Grandma bouncing along in a covered wagon. It's all been so sentimentalized. On TV, quilts have become nothing but cheery symbols of family. So when you say 'quilt artist' you sometimes see people roll their eyes a bit. But things are changing—fast. Those eye rollers would be surprised to hear just how much interest there is out there in the kind of quilt I make." ✩

THE RIBBON QUILT

IT CAN BE FASCINATING to analyze how a quiltmaker borrowed an idea from here, an aesthetic from there, and put them all together in a new way to come up with something unexpected and absolutely gorgeous. Here we have a quilt entirely constructed of silk ribbons—a rare and beautiful object to be sure, but fitting neatly into no known genre of quilt making. How did it come to be? To make an educated guess, we must deconstruct it one step at a time, imagining what its maker must have been looking at, what her influences were, what she would have been reading and thinking as she began to plan her quilt sometime during the last half of the nineteenth century.

If she happened to be a reader of *Godey's Lady's Book* (And who wasn't? It was the bible of fashion and home decoration for American women from 1830 through 1898) she might have gotten the idea for a silk quilt from its pages. From the 1850s on, *Godey's* advocated silk, and the English template system for constructing silk patterns, suggesting that pieces of fabric should be basted around a paper template pattern before being sewn together. If our maker was a fan of *Frank Leslie's Magazine* she might have followed the advice of a Mrs. Pullans, imported from England to be that periodical's "director of the worktable." Mrs. P. dismissed cotton quilts as "valueless" and in her 1859 opus, *The Lady's Manual of Fancywork,* encouraged women to make quilts in silks, satins, and velvets. Template patterns published in periodicals

during the 1850s included a basketweave pattern and others similar to those on this quilt.

Our maker may have begun with these mid-century ideas and added a "modern" touch—delicate, weblike embroidery. During the 1870s and 1880s, fancy stitching became de rigueur for quiltmakers, as women rushed to decorate the fashionable silk and velvet patchwork throws known as Crazy Quilts. Embroidered flowers embellished black velvet expanses, while cobwebby stitchery joined patch to patch, uniting a whole, apparently aimlesss pattern of silk and velvet bits in a lacy, visual armature. Ladies used every stitch in their arsenal—from the briar or feather stitch to the plush stitch—the fancier the better. While our maker has clearly rejected the "crazy" aesthetic, she does not seem adverse to using a little needlework to relieve her geometric simplicity. In some of the blocks diganonal lines of ribbons are connected with openwork embroidery executed in exactly the same shade as the ribbons, while in other blocks, tiny crosses and rosettes in contrasting colors finish off the pattern.

Those colors are themselves quite interesting, for about this same time Crazy Quilt makers began to avail themselves of the silk ribbons, free for the taking, tied around every bundle of cigars their husbands and brothers bought at the corner store. Usually made in rich shades of gold, and often printed in blue and maroon, these silky morsels made perfect embellishments for Crazy Quilts and were also stacked into log cabin–style patterns, forming entire quilts. Our maker has used no cigar ribbons at all, and yet to those who study such things, her

With its unexpected colors and satiny textures this Victorian Ribbon quilt adds richness to the mix of patterns in an English–style room.

coloration would look eerily familiar—such a preponderance of gold, set off with dull maroons and blues,
even a little cigar brown thrown in here and there.
Perhaps she unconsciously planned her color scheme
according to the ribbons she saw bundled around her
brother's stogies and incorporated into her sister-in-
law's quilts.

There, however, the similarities end. Unlike cigar
premiums, the "ribbons" that make up this quilt have no
identity of their own. They may not even be ribbons in
the technical sense—merely narrow strips of silk and
satin. They are there to connect, to line up, to weave
themselves into the various patterns that block by block
make up this quilt. It is really more like a sampler quilt
constructed, as an aide-mémoire, with samples of patterns to be used in future quilts or simply to show off
an extensive repertoire—using silk ribbon instead
of triangles and squares of calico. Although patterns are
repeated several times in various colorways, there are at
least twelve different ones represented, and they are all
intricate and beautiful.

Perhaps our lady was young during the "silken"
1850s, and a comfortable matron during the "crazy"
1870s and 1880s. Perhaps she made this quilt in the
1890s—a culmination of all she had seen and learned
during a long life of quiltmaking. Perhaps she put it
together her own way, cherished and preserved it, to be
passed down to our own time. Perhaps. ✩

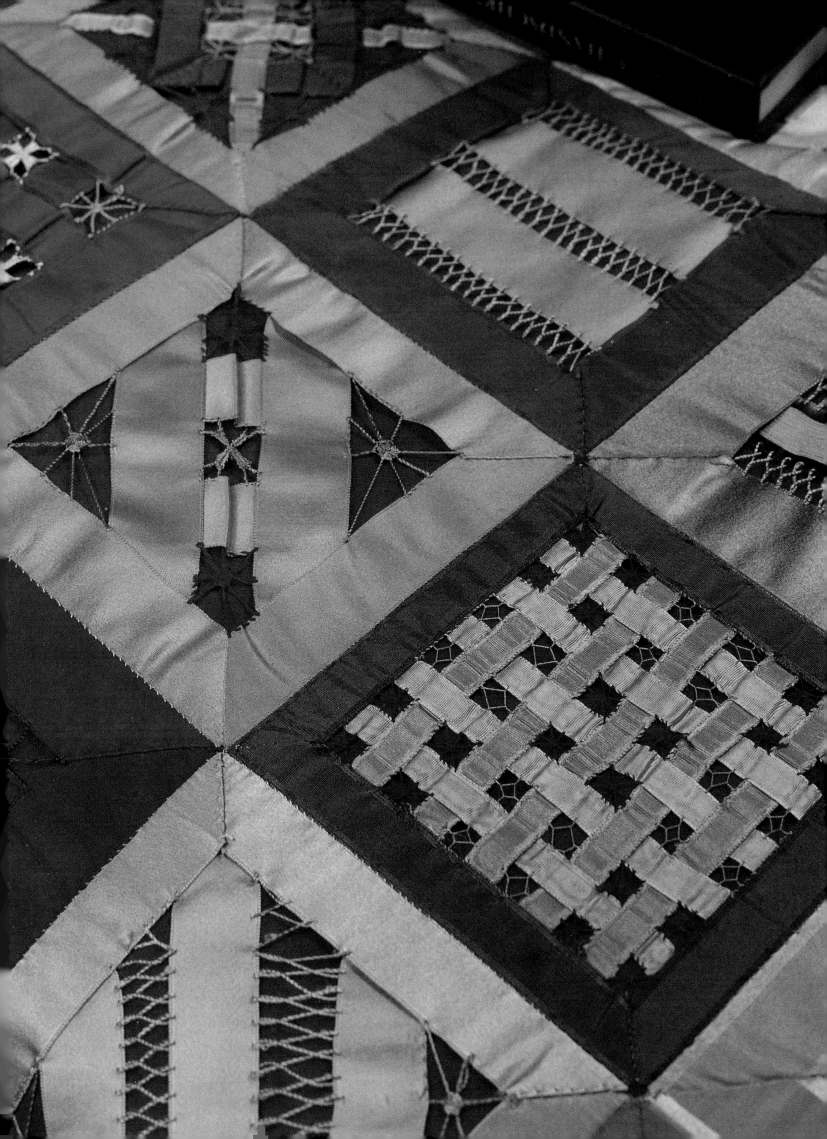

THE
INDIGO &
WHITE
PINEAPPLE
QUILT

DEEP BLUE AND WHITE. Historically, these are a magical combination—the colors of great Chinese porcelain, classic delft pottery, and flowing toile de Jouy. When it comes to American quilts, however, the combination is so effective and familiar that we may not realize how difficult it was to achieve. Throughout most of the nineteenth century, the production of a convenient, effective, colorfast blue dye remained problematic. Ancient and Medieval European dyers had resorted to the fermentation of woad leaves, part of the mustard family, to produce an acceptably colorfast blue. In the sixteenth century, indigo, a plant native to both Europe and the Americas, supplanted woad (although the latter also continued to be used until the mid-nineteenth century).

Indigo was an improvement, but it was still difficult to work with. It was time-consuming and expensive as one hundred pounds of plant material were required to produce just four ounces of dye. In a long and tedious production process, the plants were harvested, steeped, fermented, and finally drained. That liquid was aerated by workers who climbed right into the tanks and beat it with paddles to create the right chemical reaction. The resulting solids were allowed to settle and were finally cut into

cubes, called junks and sold as indigo dye. Another problem then arose: Unlike many natural dyes, indigo is not water-soluble and cannot easily be used to form a liquid in which fabric can be dipped. A complicated process was required to form such a potion, which then needed to evaporate completely before the color would be set in the fabric. To create patterns, certain areas of fabric were painted with wax to resist the dye. Various hues could be achieved by redying specified areas.

Although synthetic indigo was finally introduced in 1897, natural indigo continued to be used well into the twentieth century. Rural Southern housewives sometimes even grew their own and processed it by means of a blue pot (a rather smelly, fermenting vessel kept as far as possible from the family dwelling place) that could be kept going indefinitely. One Southern country woman knows of a pot that was in continuous use for ninety-four years. Most quilters however, preferred to buy their blue-and-white fabrics and as early as the mid-nineteenth century, had a huge selection at their disposal. Textile mills were printing literally thousands of different blue-and-white designs, offered by convenient mail-order as well as retail shops.

This variety was due at least in part to the popularity of blue and white among quilters who, during the last half of the nineteenth century, used it more frequently than any other combination. Some quilt historians have suggested that its popularity was due in part to the influence of the Women's Christian Temperance Union (an organization dedicated to fighting the evils of alcohol) whose colors were blue and white. Whatever their political stance, many mid- to late-nineteeteenth-century quilters attempted at least one example and often embellished it with their fanciest quilting. The simplicity and elegance of the classic combination helped quilters refine and manipulate traditional designs and made them stand out in bold relief. In this reverse white-on-indigo blue quilt from 1870, for example, the Pineapple pattern can be seen in all of its graphic symmetry. Almost twenty different blue-and-white fabrics were used to make this quilt top, but the result is anything but busy. Fine, dense quilting, both geometric and floral, adds another subtle, decorative touch.

Although often abstracted to almost pinecone proportions, the pineapple remains a highly significant motif in quiltmaking. According to popular folklore, nineteenth-century sea captains impaled the distinctive tropical fruit on their gateposts to announce their return home from exotic lands, so it became a symbol of hospitality, of welcome and good fellowship. Not surprisingly, this attractive motif soon turned up in many of the decorative arts—including furniture made by leading American cabinetmakers, and of course in the patterns of classic American quilts.

A classic combination, blue and white is paired with an elegant, allover pattern and allowed to become the focus of a calm, airy bedroom.

This pattern possesses a fascinating, illusional quality that can make you blink in surprise. To see the illusion, read the pineapples as a circle around a diamond, then as a cross. Voila! The geometric, stairstep shape of the pineapples tells us that this pattern is related to the famous Log Cabin family. But while these pineapples are indeed made up of narrow "logs," the pattern as a whole incorporates other shapes, producing a different overall appearance. In deep blue and white it's unforgettable—a classic that is as traditional or as modern as we need it to be. ✡

ROYAL
HAWAIIAN
FLAG
QUILT

THIS IMPRESSIVE QUILT looks as if it belongs in the Great Hall of the Duke of Earl's country seat in Yorkshire. Interestingly, it was made in the Hawaiian islands in about 1928. Hawaii has a surprisingly long and rich tradition of quiltmaking, beginning with the introduction of cotton cloth by missionary wives around 1820. Hawaiian girls were duly instructed in quilting and other domestic arts, and quilts soon replaced the native mulberry bark coverlets. Warmth was certainly not a priority and piecing did not particularly appeal to the Hawaiians—why cut out small bits only to put them together to form something larger?—but fancy appliqué caught on immediately. Native quilters began to create exquisite patterns based on native flora and other designs, usually appliquéd in a single color over white, and surrounded them with elaborate echo quilting, repeating the outlines of the pattern. The Hawaiian quilt became a distinctive genre—highly prized—and never duplicated in any other locale.

In 1843 Hawaiians put their new quilting skills to another use—the declaration of patriotic, monarchistic fervor. Having been discovered by the British Captain Cook in 1778, Hawaii was officially claimed by the British navy for Britain in 1843. The Union Jack flew over the islands for only five months before sovereignty was returned to the Hawaiian king, but that was long enough for islanders to begin to make the striking quilts that would become known as the *Ku'u Hae Aloha* or the *Lost Beloved Flag*. When, in the 1890s, the United States annexed Hawaii and the reigning monarch, Queen Liliuokalani, abdicated, the Royal Hawaiian flag was again lowered, this time forever—precipitating a huge burst of similar quiltmaking, a mourning of the end of the Hawaiian kingdom.

For a people said to resent the British takeover of 1843, Hawaiians seemed surprisingly eager to continue a symbolic association with all things British. The Royal Hawaiian flag sports a Union Jack in its corner, and the coat of arms of the Hawaiian monarch is a dead ringer for those boasted by the higher English aristocrats— if you overlook the floral "lei" floating underneath. Perhaps Hawaiian flag designers felt that anything less than traditionally regal—by Western standards—would not be afforded proper international respect. At any rate, a typical Royal Hawiian quilt is composed of four elongated Hawaiian flags (one for each of the island kingdoms) surrounding a central, suitably Royal motif. The flags originally had seven stripes (each representing a major island), but with the addition of the island of Kauai in 1870, the number went up to eight. This change should have been a convenient dating device but as quilt historians warn, it is notoriously unreliable. Some Hawaiian quilters arbitrarily inserted up to ten stripes simply to balance their compositions.

In this particular example two of the flags are "flying" upside down—said to symbolize the displeasure of

This Royal Hawaiian quilt recalls the years when Hawaii was still a proud monarchy and represents the islands' surprisingly active quilting tradition.

the last queen at being dethroned by the Americans. Each has eight stripes done in channel quilting. The central appliquéd coat of arms is backed in rich red and surmounted by another crown and an "ermine" cape, further symbolizing the traditional trappings of royalty. This central motif is surrounded by intricate, typically Hawaiian echo quilting. Its rich gold color sets off the red, white, and blue of the flags while the overall linear design, punctuated with radiating Union Jacks, pleases the eye as it leads it inexorably to the center.

The warm, humid Hawaiian climate was murderous on textiles of any kind—hastening normal deterioration and necessitating a peculiar kind of preservation: When a maker saw a beloved quilt beginning to go, she simply copied it in new fabrics—continuing the cycle for another generation or two. It is rare, therefore, to find any Hawaiian quilt that dates back before 1870. This 1928 version may have been based on a design originally executed many years previously. We are lucky to be seeing it at all. Although most native quilters made at least one Royal Hawaiian Flag quilt during their lifetimes, few of these heraldic masterpieces ever made it to the mainland. In addition to the conservation problem and the natural tendency for proud Hawaiians to hold on to symbols of their royal heritage, there is the matter of the *mana*. According to Hawaiian lore, the *mana* or spirit of the quiltmaker is believed to live in a finished quilt. Some makers, therefore, specified that their quilts be burned at their deaths. Others wouldn't let them out of their sight. Liliuokalani would have been proud. ✩

THE PRINCESS STAR QUILT

No other style of quilt packs quite the same graphic wallop as a great four-block. It's a simple, highly successful formula: A design block interesting enough to stand on its own is repeated four times, positioned in such a way that a larger quilt-wide pattern is created—one even more stunning than the four parts. Each block must carry its substantial sector (it's a quarter of the quilt, after all) yet relate perfectly to its neighbors. Each must be a star—and a team player. This fortuitous patterning method got its start about 1820. Before then whole cloth quilts were the rule—often featuring center medallions surrounded by secondary borders and floral sprays. When repeating block quilts came into fashion, quilters began to divide the quilt top geometrically, first in quarters, creating a four-block, then into nine segments for the nine-patch, and so on.

The four-block quilt was brought to its full flowering in the mid-nineteenth century by Pennsylvanians of German extraction. Attracted by William Penn's colony, Southern Germans settled Lancaster County in the seventeenth century in such numbers that they soon made up a third of the population and became known as the Pennsylvania Deutsche, or Dutch. As part of their German heritage they brought with them the art of ornamental paper-cutting *(scherenschmitte),* the source for the charming appliqué and pieced patterns found in their nineteenth-century quilts. These were soon spread throughout the state and beyond, disseminated by tinkers and traveling tin salesmen who bartered pierced and cut tin stencils for food and lodging. Unlike many other pieced and even appliqué formats, the four-block quilt often called for rather large pieces of fabric. Luckily, Lancaster County's proximity to the port of Philadelphia and other textile sources solved that problem, even in the earliest years.

While a quintessential example of a Lancaster County four-block, this quilt, ca. 1880, is made even more dazzling by its Mennonite provenance. The Mennonites, a peace-loving, unworldly, highly communal sect that originated in Switzerland during the Reformation, were among those seventeenth-century Germans who settled in Pennsylvania. There they have remained for three centuries, living among their "English" neighbors from whom they quickly learned, and then perfected, the

With its Old World Germanic design and bold coloration, this Pennsylvania Mennonite quilt brings instant drama to any interior.

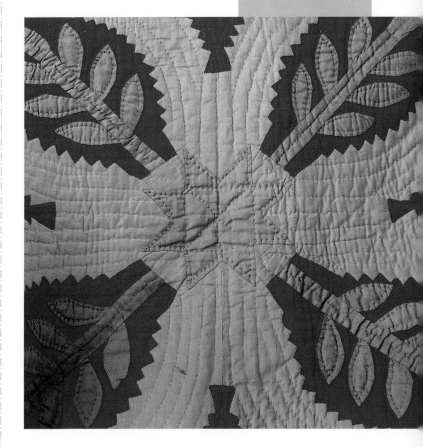

art of quilting. To their predilection for the drama of the four-block, their stock of Pennsylvania Dutch patterns, and their advanced skill with the needle, Mennonite quilters added their own unique color sense, untainted by long exposure to popular culture—starting with backgrounds of yellow and red, then adding pink, orange, and other colors of unusual values and hues.

In the pattern department, Mennonite quilters were not afraid of experimentation either. In fact, this one, Princess Star Feather, is a variation of a variation. The popular pattern upon which it was based, Princess Feather, was based on an even earlier emblem—three feathers attached to a crown, the personal insignia of the Prince of Wales. Horticulturalists named a flower Prince's Feather after this motif and quilters borrowed it, slurred its spelling, and gave it a swirling, curving shape, half flower, half star, that seems to be constantly in motion, ready to whirl right off the quilt top. This quilter has quieted that motion by turning some of the flower's petals around to face each other. Now the shape is more like a star.

A true eight-point star is at the center of each larger star and oak leaves, a symbol of happiness and long life, are visible between their curving points. The center juxtaposition of these points creates its own secondary pattern that joins the four main shapes and helps unify the entire quilt. The stars, the oak leaves, the tiny tulips in urns, as well as the border of triangles that defines the four-block field, are all typical of the Pennsylvania German four-block style, but as usual its Mennonite maker has skewed her colors away from the expected. Sea foam green is combined with mustard and set upon a background darker than either color—a soft brick red. These choices and the large, dramatic graphics of the four block format itself free our vision—pushing the pattern beyond its folksy repetoire of stars and tulips and into the wider world of pure design. ✩

THE MOTHER-IN-LAW QUILT

MRS. LULU BENNETT was a bit of a card. Born in 1885 in rural Illinois, she was married at eighteen in St. Louis, Missouri, and became in short order, the mother of four children, a talented dress designer, a quiltmaker, a songwriter, a poet, and an intrepid contest entrant. With such a myriad of talents she became something of a local celebrity, but through it all never lost the ability to laugh at herself—or to turn that humor to good use. Judging from her reputation, Lulu was probably much funnier than the following joke, which she heard on the radio one day in 1930, but its old-fashioned, vaudevillian humor stuck in her mind. One man says to the other: "I cut off my dog's tail this morning." The other man says: "Why did you do that?" The first man answers: "Because I don't want him wagging his tail and showing how happy he is when my mother-in-law comes up the walk!"

Lulu was a mother-in-law herself, and as she was on perfectly friendly terms with her son's wife, created this slyly amusing, pictorial quilt and presented it to her with a flourish. In it the family dog, his stump of a tail ominously still, sits on the front steps of a house, awaiting the arrival of the hatted lady striding purposefully toward him. A discreetly embroidered panel nearby reads: "The home that tenderly greets the

This 1930s pictorial quilt combines the homey warmth of the American folk art tradition with the cool shapes and colors of Art Deco.

mother-in-law." In addition to this bit of gentle sarcasm, Lulu dropped other hints to make sure the viewer understood the joke: The mother-in-law is dressed in a tacky granny getup complete with a handbag worthy of the Queen Mother. This funereal outfit is completely at odds with the cheery, pastel dwelling she is stalking—she looks for all the world like the Bad Fairy at the wedding of the princess.

This is a story in a glance—told by Lulu Bennett, not with paint on canvas, but in a textile tableau requiring both skill with a needle and considerable aesthetic acumen. The fine, cross-hatched quilting is the perfect overall choice—simulating the house's brickwork and even the shingles on the roof. Deep yellow cottons appliquéd in the windows produce a bright, welcoming aura, while the house's front walk, projecting toward the viewer, establishes correct perspective. At first glance the trees, unusual bushlike forms, appear to be a cop-out by Lulu, who clearly used three large, appliquéd leaves (possibly leftover from some other quilt) to make them. But look again: These trees are quite graceful and decorative and with their carefully embroidered bark, echo the slightly Deco look of the stylized flowers in the foreground. It's as if Lulu were reminding herself: "Don't make it all look too real—this is supposed to be funny."

Lulu can't take all the credit for the memorable color palette. Her pale, creamy colors are typical of many quilts made during the 1930s—the same ones found in the floaty dresses of the reigning screen goddesses. However, the municipal green of the foreground and gray blue of the background are particularly well chosen, as is the butterscotch color of the roof and walk.

The prairie point border was made by folding squares into small, exact triangles and then inserting them between the layers of the quilt before the final finishing. This was a fashionable way of framing a quilt during the first half of the twentieth century.

When Lulu picked up her needle, pictorial quilts—those that tell a story or use specific visual imagery—were fairly rare. The American quilting tradition was built on medallion-style florals, multiblock albums, and allover patterns that stunned with their graphic power. Sprinkled throughout the nineteenth century, a few quilters did use pictorial images to tell stories from the Bible or their own tales, but such attempts were unusual. Even by Lulu's day, not much had changed. Contestants in the 1933 Century of Progress quilt contest turned to pictorials to commemorate the technological progress of the United States but when it came to winning medals, they were routed by makers who had stuck to tried-and-true allover patterning. It was not until recently that the quilt medium began to be considered important for artists who create single-composition, pictorial works. Now a whole generation is producing such quilts, both objective and abstract. Not only is their work accepted, it is considered the most significant in late-twentieth-century quilting.

Lulu Bennett lived to see it all happen (she died in 1979) but she probably wasn't surprised. She surely knew the rest of the world would catch up with her someday. ☆

THE ANIMAL CRAZY QUILT

THE YEAR THIS UNIQUE Crazy Quilt was made, the fad for Crazies was at its peak. It was 1885 and enthusiastic needlewomen were creating standard versions of that High Victorian creation, by the thousands. One New York family of the period was said to have turned out three quilts, several throw pillows, a number of table scarves, and a piano cover, and was contemplating further production. Crazies were an adventure, an imaginative exercise in textile art, gloriously unfettered by the stark, predictable geometry of other quilt patterns. They were also a challenge to make: The editor of *Harper's Bazaar* wrote in 1882: "Now we are very daring. We go boldly on without any design at all." But in fact, Crazies were among the most carefully designed of all quilts. Makers quickly discovered that it was quite a task to take unrelated scraps of luxurious fabric, put them together in apparently random order, and come out with something that looked like it had been there, all in one delicious piece, all along.

Many quilts achieved this "oneness" with decorative embroidery positioned at strategic intervals. This lacy overlay visually united the random pattern of dark velvets and silks beneath. The over-the-top decorative quality of the Crazy seemed to cry out for the most elaborate forms of embroidery and other handiwork. Contemporary manuals recommended the inclusion of such exotics as Kensington shaded embroidery, outline work, appliquéd plush and satinwork, not to mention beadwork, *point Russe*, feather and herringbone stitching, and ribbon and tinsel embroidery.

Of course, not everybody could embroider beautifully, much less design the lilies, fans and characters from fairy stories and nursery rhymes that Crazy Quilt makers preferred. By the mid-1880s, silk and thread companies were stepping into the gap, offering patterns for embroidered motifs and even finished pieces which could be immediately incorporated into one's quilt. The same companies were also happy to provide painted, quilt-ready motifs, and should one's supply of velvet scraps dwindle, to sell quilters packaged remnants in a wide choice of fabric and color. Ironically, this commercialization spelled the end of the fad these companies had hoped to prolong. By 1887 the magazine editors who had sung the praises of the Crazy just ten years before had turned their backs on its velvety excesses: "Too awful for words," sniffed *Godey's Lady's Book*. Crazies ceased to be cutting edge quilting design but remained part of the standard repertoire of active quilters all over the country.

Even the jaded editors of *Godey's* would probably not have objected to this example. Its maker seems to have borrowed the organization of the Crazy Quilt but not its aesthetic. The varied palette of the Crazy—in which black is often the unifier—has been keyed down here to a few muted colors. The areas of gray, taupe, and brown are fairly large and are separated with uncharacteristically large areas of white. This is

With its stylized shapes and muted colors, this rare Animal Crazy Quilt would be a welcome addition to any interior, from High Victorian to Swedish Modern.

really a rather modern color scheme, the kind you'd expect to see paired with Knoll furniture in Beverly Hills. Well, almost. One dark red strawberry near the center is a clear refugee from Victoriana, but it seems placed there to point up the contrast between what we expect and what we are actually seeing. Furthermore, the appliquéd and embroidered animals are not much like the sentimental illustrations in Victorian fairy tales. These stylized, graceful leaping stags and running horses are much closer to the Art Deco—a style that was not to arrive on the landscape for another forty years.

Every denizen of nature—birds, insects, fruit, flowers—seems chosen for its charming shape. Some look like origami creations (perhaps this maker made it to the Centennial Exhibition in Philadelphia in 1876, which showcased Asian design), others look like cave paintings or American primitives. The maker was careful to leave plenty of open space in which to view each creature or flower. Fancy stitching is understated and there is no froufrou border. Its a real tour de force, perhaps the work of many years. Its owner, a collector who has seen thousands of quilts over the years, has never seen another one remotely like it. ✩

THE
"TALK
DIRTY TO ME,
HONEY"
QUILT

"I'VE ALWAYS LIKED nineteenth century imagery," says Texas quilt artist Rachel K. Turner. "People think the Victorian era was stuffy but it was actually very lively and romantic." A longtime admirer of American illustrators Charles Dana Gibson and Joseph Leyendecker (think Gibson Girl and the Arrow Shirt Collar Man) as well as the forgotten advertising artists of that gaslit era, Turner likes to incorporate their aesthetic into her work. She also likes to explore gender issues. What she doesn't like is to take herself too seriously. So it is not surprising that the chance discovery of a cache of camp, high Victorian dental imagery, plus the memory of a familiar phrase, would have sparked the creation of a quilt, memorably entitled *Talk Dirty to Me, Honey*.

Turner's quilt pleases and amuses on many levels at once. With its geometric grid enclosing a series of shapely ovals and circles—executed in a variety of beiges and reds that somehow meld into a cohesive palette—*Talk Dirty to Me, Honey* displays the graphic power of the allover patterning that has delighted so many generations. But instead of late-nineteenth-century loops and triangles, Turner's geometrics are actually a pictorial pastiche of that era's advertising; her quilt can be read as a giant brick wall against which row after row of posters proclaim the superiority of a dentist, a den-

ture maker, or a tooth powder. Like one of those illusionary quilts in which patterns seem to change shape depending on how you look at them, Turner's pictorial parody seems to go in and out of focus, turning effortlessly from a Mondrianesque grid to a Victorian placard and back again. Meanwhile, when viewed in repetitive splendor, these sets of gaping teeth become a bit ridiculous—as ridiculous as Turner clearly finds the male request that is the quilt's title.

"All my quilts have kind of an edge to them," says Turner. "I find it challenging to use the quilt medium to say the things I want to say— many of which have to do with the relationship between the sexes." (She has created another quilt in

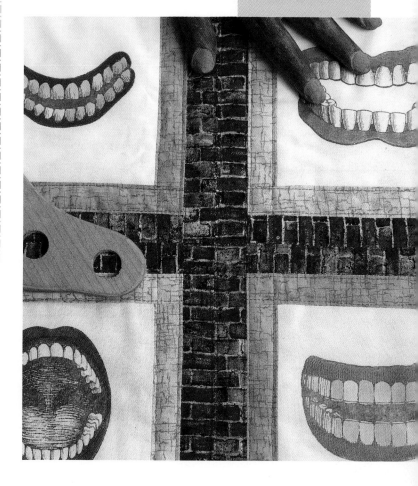

Emphasizing the linear shape of the dining table even as it provides texture and color, Rachel K. Turner's humorous quilt is also a guaranteed ice breaker for a dinner party.

which every block contains a bold staring eye. Title? An ironic: *I Only Have Eyes for You*.) A third-generation amateur needlewoman who has always made her own clothes, Turner studied art and became a professional printmaker, turning out "intaglio prints, lithographs, everything." Quiltmaking was a natural artistic segue—a perfect way to combine her two interests. However, after determining that the quilt was to be her preferred medium she faced the usual challenge of converting the rest of the world. "It took me two years to convince my department at the University of Tennessee that this was art," she laughs. "Quilts were still seen as something that you put on the bed. But I finally got my BFA in studio art as a quiltmaker."

In *Talk Dirty to Me, Honey* Turner utilized her print-making skills, making photocopies of images found in nineteenth-century source materials and soaking them in acetone. By laying an acetone-soaked photocopy on a block of muslin and running it through a press, sharp, clear images of Victorian teeth were transferred to each of the twenty-four quilt blocks. Employing another artistic skill, Turner hand-painted the transfers, pre-serving the authentic Victorian feeling in her coloration. Before printing, the blocks of muslin were tea-stained to achieve the proper "old" background shade and were afterwards assembled into a grid, surrounded by strips of an amusing brick-printed fabric—stained and bleached to a proper Victorian agedness. This printed masonry also forms the entire back of the quilt, contin-uing the illusion of the quilt as placarded wall.

"This is an old tradition," says Turner of quiltmaking. "But the way it is being done now it is also very new. You have to get past all the baggage about people's grand-mothers and use it to say what you want to say. You should see another quilt I've made," she continues, "the one that laces together like a corset." ✫

AMISH
DIAMOND
IN THE
SQUARE
QUILT

THE AMISH QUILTS of Lancaster County, Pennsylvania are the downtown sophisticates of the quilt world. A roomful of these masterpieces looks uncannily like a gallery hung with multimillion dollar abstract paintings. Constructed in simple, geometric patterns in deep, saturated colors chosen and arranged with unfailing precison, these quilts pack the kind of aes-thetic punch that makes collectors of contemporary art sigh and reach for their checkbooks. It's a look that attracts squadrons of BMWs to Sunday flea markets in Lancaster County, and caused prices of Amish quilts to rise faster than prices of almost any other kind of quilts—particu-larly after the 1971 exhibition, "Abstract Design in American Quilts," a smash hit at New York's Whitney Museum of American Art. But looks can be deceiving. Amish quilts may look like the work of world-famous modern artists like Mark Rothko and Joseph Albers, but when Amish women created these quilts between 1890 and 1940, modernity—even art—was the farthest thing from their minds.

The Amish deliberately turn away from many aspects of modern life and eschew nonfunctional vanities like "art." It has been this way since the 1690s when the

Like a great 1960s colorfield painting, this Amish quilt stuns with simplicity and the juxtapo-sition of its dense, saturated colors.

followers of Jacob Amman, an Alsatian bishop, splintered off from other Mennonite sects to practice an even more conservative Protestantism that included separation from one's neighbors, discipline, simplicity in dress and decoration, and strict conformation to the rules of the community. Arriving in America in the eighteenth century, the Amish made their way to Pennsylvania's Lancaster Country, and later to Ohio, Indiana, and fifteen other states, where they live to this day—fascinating fellow citizens who, following their own road, continue to cruise Lancaster county byways in horse-drawn buggies.

Quilting is not a traditional Amish practice and was probably adopted from their more worldy "English" neighbors late in the nineteenth century. Using the plain, dark wools in which they dressed, the Lancaster County Amish (among the most conservative of Amish communities) avoided charges of vanity by deliberately choosing "old-fashioned" patterns long discarded by their more fashion-conscious neighbors. The medallion styles they favored are a clear throwback to the late eighteenth and early nineteenth centuries. Respecting their community's preferences for conformity, almost all quilters used the same wide borders and simple designs like Sunshine and Shadow, Bars, Center Square, and Diamond in the Square (of which this one—in crimson, purple, and spring green, and featuring many different quilting designs—is a stunning example). No patterned fabric of any kind was allowed to enliven the mix. It sounds like a recipe for quilting disaster and yet these quilts are anything but dull.

The wool fabrics chosen by Amish quiltmakers absorb rather than reflect light, resulting in deep, rich tones. With no white background separating them, these dense, saturated purples, wines, teals, and reds resonate strongly against each other—changing our perception of individual colors and creating memorable harmonies that seem inevitable once they exist. As Amish women had little background in art history and few chances to experiment with color in other areas of their lives, this innate sense of tone and hue is a happy mystery. Their superb needlework skills, exhibited on the wide exapnses of pure color typical of their quilts, comes as no surprise as Amish women honed those skills making clothes for their families. This subtle, practical form of quilt decoration—hearts, birds, flowers, and designs of every description hidden in an apparently plain expanse, contributed to a more durable whole and was typical of the Amish way.

Quilting flourished in Amish communities long after other American women, distracted by prohibition and woman's suffrage, had laid down their thimbles. Such burning issues went largely unnoticed in Lancaster County, where home sewing continued unabated and, in the absence of drive-ins and bridge parties, quilting remained a popular communal acitivity. Even today quiltmaking continues to be an important Lancaster Amish industry, but it has become more self-conscious and employs many synthetic materials. The golden age of Amish quilting ended before mid-century.

That the Amish quilt is largely a twentieth-century phenomenon, chronologically parallel to the rise of geometric modern art, has added to its myth as a sort of aesthetic blood brother to the likes of Mark Rothko. But while artists like Rothko worked all their lives to reduce their work to its elemental form, the Amish just did what came naturally. As Robert Shaw points out in *Quilts: A Living Tradition*, "Amish quilts proceed from the place modern artists seek to find." ✩

LOG CABIN
BARN- RAISING
QUILT

IF YOU HAD TO PICK one pattern that would symbolize all of nineteenth-century American quiltmaking, odds are you'd end up with some version of a Log Cabin quilt. No other pattern has been so popular for so long. None is as versatile nor as quintessentially American, as simple yet visually challenging. Consisting of fabric "logs" organized into blocks, the Log Cabin system can be used to form an almost infinite number of striking, allover designs. Born during the third quarter of the century when quiltmaking was at its height, this family of patterns quickly became so popular that nearly every serious quilter made at least one during a lifetime. So fascinating were the changes that occurred in the pattern when the colors and the placement of logs were altered that she often made a dozen.

But first she had to learn how. The Log Cabin technique is unusual —a specific hybrid of appliqué and piecing known as pressed piecing, which took some practice. First, hundreds of fabric rectangles or logs had to be prepared. Early Log Cabin quilts were made mostly from wools like challis or richly colored cottons. These were followed by the silk and velvet log cabins of the Victorian era, and finally by the pastels of the Depression. Next, the quilter prepared a foundation

Log Cabin pattern quilts like this Barn-Raising variation get much of their graphic power from light and dark fabric strips arranged for maximum contrast.

block of some useful material like muslin or gabardine and basted the very first piece of the quilt—not a log at all, but a square—right into the middle of the first block. This block was known as the "hearth" or "chimney"—the symbolic, frequently red, heart of the two-dimensional "log house" the quilter would soon be building. The first log would then be pieced onto a side of the square, pressed flat, and then covered with the edge of the next log, which would then be pressed, and so on and so on. Every raw edge would be covered by the next piece.

When the entire block of muslin had been painstakingly covered with logs it would be laid aside to wait for the completion of all of the other blocks. The quilt was formed by sewing these finished blocks side by side, so that the carefully arranged light and dark logs formed a memorable allover pattern. Fortunately, the finished product needed no quilting: The presence of so many seams obviated the need for more structural support.

With this example, created around 1880, the Pennsylvania quilter used a variety of plain and printed cottons and calicoes to form a "barn-raising" version of the Log Cabin pattern. What a stunner! Our eye looks, and then looks again, reading the darks and lights as almost three-dimensional, with the darks forming a visual "overlay" that seems closer to us than the lighter colors "underneath." There is no central hearth, although individual hearths are plainly represented by squares of the traditional red in the center of every block. Instead, four blocks come together at the center of the quilt to form a dark center diamond. But this can also be read as a cross—part of the rising barn scaffolding from which the pattern takes its name.

The whole has been surrounded with something that resembles a traditional picture frame—complete with an inner liner. This broad, simple frame is the perfect complement to the busy geometry of the center. Throughout, the quilt's sophisticated colors bring to mind the unusual palette that would be used by Amish quiltmakers in the same geographical area in the decades to come. ✩

THE
"WHEN THE BEE STINGS"
QUILT

JUST LOOKING AT THE LIST of techniques Joan Lintault uses in the making of her quilts makes the observer feel quite exhausted—and impressed. Such a list leads off with fabric dyeing and continues through screen-printing, fabric painting, appliqué, piecing, and quilting. "I do not choose to reject a technique simply because it is laborious," says this veteran Illinois quilt-maker, adding with characteristic humor: "I base my work on geological rather than TV time." It shows. Lintault's quilts can seem almost miraculous in their conception and execution—entire imaginative worlds in microcosm that rivet our attention and keep us there looking, discovering layer upon layer of intricate detail.

Lintault's love affair with textiles began a few decades ago in the Bronx, far away from her current midwestern home. There, her dressmaker grandmother filled the young girl's house with a tempting stash of left-over fabric. Lintault was immediately attracted, but when she went to college to study art, she was urged to concentrate on the more conventional fields of screen printing, weaving, and ceramics—the field in which Lintault finally recieved her master's degree. Then, in the 1960s, Lintault remembers: "I went to an auction. They were selling quilts and I looked at them and thought 'I can do better than that.' I gradually migrated into fabric."

But not just any kind. Not only has Lintault always disliked the idea that someone else's quilt might contain exactly the same fabric as her own, but she feels strongly that everything she does should make a contribution to the total design. Store-bought is therefore out of the question. So begins the laborious processes that ultimately lead to quilts like *When the Bee Stings.* To make this quilt, Lintault explains, "I start with white muslin —bleached or unbleached. I wash it, dye it, spray color over it, steam it, wash and iron it, screen-print it, and then hand-paint it." Lintault then cuts out the desired shapes and begins to pin them up on a design board. Unlike most quilters, she does not use a backing. Each piece is sewn to the next—in a process that falls

Massed with the variegated shapes and hues of nature, Joan Lintault's When the Bee Stings *is the modern equivalent of a medieval tapestry —bringing warmth, texture, and color to the room.*

between appliqué and piecing—and then quilted. Occasionally she leaves holes (like the honeycomb in this quilt, for example.) "I'm not interested in making something solid just for its own sake," she says.

Yet Lintault has much in common with the generations of quilters who have preceded her, including making quilts that represent her own life and interests. *When the Bee Stings* is Lintault's paean to the cycles of nature, a fascination that blossomed a decade ago when she went to Japan on a Fulbright grant to study fabric dyeing. She became sharply aware of that country's glorious history of landscape and flower painting, and when she returned home began "to pay attention to my own little garden—my own little strip of paradise—noticing what came up when. I also noticed that bees have a lot to do with what happens there." In this quilt, busy, stinging insects are also a metaphor for the realization that danger lurks everywhere—even in paradise. Indeed,

In her fabric depiction of a bountiful still life, Joan Lintault has broken free of the medium's traditional boundaries by including transparent lace inserts and three-dimensional vegetables.

the boiling circle of bees at the center of *When the Bee Stings* is both beautiful and slightly sinister—a perfect foil for the cheery perfection of Lintault's richly massed blossoms. "Many of my quilts have hints of danger in them," she says.

THE "GIVE US THIS DAY" QUILT

GIVE US THIS DAY displays Lintault's idiosyncratic use of negative space—here represented by inserts of lace "tablecloth" supporting a still life of almost cosmic proportions. The artist mined all periods of art history for still life painting—from Roman wall painting, through the Renaissance and beyond. "There's everyone from Frida Kahlo to Giuseppe Arcimboldo in there," says Lintault, adding that the prominent loaf of bread is another reminder of her own life. "I made my own bread for a while," says she simply, "and that's what it looked like." Nearby, a juicy bunch of individually stuffed carrots catches the eye. Bunched together they form a three-dimensional element much like a bas-relief, their solidity an effective contrast to the transparency of the tablecloth beneath. All of this bounty is yet another slice of paradise, Lintault style. "I want to bring perpetual summer indoors," she says of her oeuvre, "the cool of the forest, the heat in the meadow, and the whine of insects in the grass." ✡

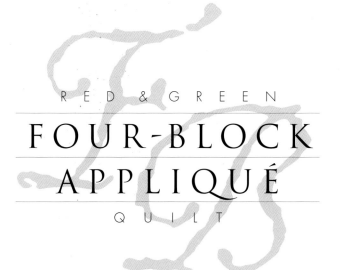

RED & GREEN

FOUR-BLOCK
APPLIQUÉ

QUILT

WHEN IN 1828 THE Scotsman David Ramsay Hay wrote a book explaining *The Laws of Harmonious Colouring,* he gave his readers two sure pathways to color-scheme heaven—harmony by anolog and harmony by contrast. The latter is, of course, the basis for this quilt's smashing red-and-green color combination. Christmas cards aside, few colors complement each other as well as these two optical opposites, and even fewer have such a long and successful history of togetherness. When it comes to quilts, red and green are practically an institution—especially when appliqué is involved: Because appliqué designs were often copied from natural forms, green was the obvious choice for leaves. Once those were in place, red just looked right for the color of the blossoms they accompanied. This may be because the combination was so familiar from earlier examples: Many of the chintzes cut out and appliquéd onto early quilts incorporated this color scheme.

All very well, but for the textile makers who supplied nineteenth-century quilters, the trick was obtaining those clear, strong reds and greens—and keeping them. Both colors presented some difficulties: Since ancient times the roots of the *Rubia tinctorum* plant had been used to make madder, which produces a brownish-red dye. Later it was discovered that a purer scarlet could be obtained from the cochineal beetle, native to Mexico and the Mediterranean. The Turks became famous for using

cochineal in a highly secret process that produced a brilliant, colorfast red dye, but it took a while before "Turkey Red" was copied successfully by Europeans and Americans. Green was an even tougher problem. A secondary color, it required the layering of blue obtained with indigo, and yellow made with natural substances like saffron, turmeric, fustic (a type of wood), or chrome (a mineral) in a rather precarious blend. As time went by, exposure to light tended to fade natural green dyes to a sort of khaki and turn chemical greens into other unexpected shades, or the yellow in the mixture would fade out entirely, leaving behind a quilt full of incongruous blue leaves.

With its traditional Pennsylvania Dutch pattern and classic red, white, and green color scheme, this four-block quilt is the quintessential folk art object—cheerful yet elegant—at home in any setting.

One of the glories of this quilt, made by an unknown quilter around 1875, is the vitality of its pure, clear green. After more than a century the color remains unfaded—a perfect harmonious complement to the vibrant Turkey red with which it was paired so many years ago. Like many examples from this period, this quilt is both pieced and appliquéd, using plain fabrics and those printed in low-contrast allover patterns that do not distract the eye. The bold, graphic, four-block format was in common use between 1830 and 1900 and was used most frequently by quilters of German extraction, especially the Pennsylvania Dutch.

In fact, anybody who is familiar with the folk art of the Pennsylvania Dutch will immediately recognize the origins of this quilt's charm. Its major motif, a bulbous tulip with its pointed petals viewed in profile, can be seen surrounding the crabbed, pointed Gothic script of Pennsylvania Dutch frakturs (decorated birth certificates and other manuscripts). It's a simple, easily recognizable shape that also appeared on the brightly painted furniture and earthenware with which quilt-makers of Germanic extraction were familiar. The eight-pointed star is also a common German motif, although here the quilter has created a rounded eight-pointed shape that looks more like a ripe, fully opened tulip than a conventional sparkler. Incorporating all of these traditional folk images, the four-block format has been used to good advantage: The quadrants of the quilt are clearly deliniated by lines of stacked triangles, but together they form a a new, quilt-wide pattern that radiates from the center and is contained by a continuous red border. Above all, this is a happy pattern—a flowery country Valentine, or a Christmas memory in which fir trees and holly berries dazzle on white snow. Pink and green simply wouldn't do. Red and green forever. ✡

THE
WAGON
WHEEL
QUILT

EVERYONE LOVES AMISH QUILTS—those deceptively simple, beautifully stitched woolen and cotton masterpieces created between 1910 and 1940. But ask a quilt fancier about Mennonite quilts and you may cause her to scratch her head a little. Although the Mennonites lived side by side with the Amish for centuries and were equally skilled producers of quilts, their quilting legend looms far less large.
The reason is simple: Most people are never quite sure whether they are looking at a Mennonite quilt—or not. The many aesthetic regulations imposed on Amish quiltmakers limiting their repertoire of patterns and materials make their work a cinch to spot, but a quilt made by the more liberal Mennonites can look a lot like other quilts. Yet, there is something about them—a heightened color sense, a level of skill—that makes us take a second look. Slowly we realize the source of Mennonite magic: Their makers took the sophisticated colorations and virtuoso quilting of the Amish and applied them to a broad range of mainstream patterns. It was a recipe for quilting dynamite.

The Amish-Mennonite connection goes back centuries before America was even a gleam in Thomas Jefferson's eye. The Mennonite sect originated in Switzerland during the Reformation, taking as its creed the

Evocative of everything from an Oriental fan to a wagon wheel, this graphic pattern is particularly effective against a rich, chocolate-brown background.

literal word of Jesus Christ. Its followers preached love, non-aggression, and separation from non-believers, but one bishop, Jacob Amman, felt that they did not go far enough. Breaking off from the original sect, he founded the Amish—a stricter version of the Mennonite church, that separated itself even further from the rest of the world. Members of both groups migrated to the United States between 1683, when German Mennonites first settled William Penn's colony, and 1874, when a large group of Russian Mennonites arrived in the Great Plains. In Lancaster County, Pennsylvania, and the Midwest, the two groups lived side by side—but often quite differently. While the Amish prohibited everything from the hanging of wallpaper to the use of motorized vehicles, Mennonites blended far more easily with their other "English" neighbors. Yet even at the wheels of their cars they remained a distinct group, looking to their churches, communities, and family structures for support and social life, concerned with the ideals of thrift, hard work, and the continuation of traditional male and female roles.

There is no better evidence of their ability to absorb the surrounding culture while remaining true to their values than a Mennonite quilt. Like the Amish, Mennonite women had learned the craft from their "English" neighbors, but their church elders put far fewer restrictions on how it could be practiced. Blessed with the pure color sense of those shielded from a daily onslaught of popular culture, Mennonite women adopted any pattern they liked and made it uniquely their own—an expression of their personalities. Encouraged by their community not to have idle hands, many became skilled needleworkers, able to produce these finely crafted, gloriously colored quilts in a wide variety of patterns. Such quilts soon became part of Mennonite culture—presented to newlyweds, used to express feelings of love and gratitude.

The owner of this pieced wool quilt knows that it was crafted around the turn of the century by a Mennonite maker. But where? We can take a guess. This is the Fan pattern, first popularized as part of Crazy Quilts and then circulated as a repeating block pattern in the late-nineteenth century. The Fan is known to have been a particular favorite of Mennonite makers in Indiana, and is found only rarely in Pennsylvania or Ohio quilts. The solid fabrics, purity of form, rich earthy colors, and complex patterning also point to this being an Indiana quilt—although we will never know for sure. We do know that it is a stunning one—combining a graphic, sophisticated, Oriental-influenced charm with a very American evocation of wagon wheels turning on a muddy, turn-of-the-century Midwest road. It's a test pattern, a decorator's color chart, a lesson in the relativity of browns. We can't take our eyes off of it. ✩

THE
PICKLE
DISH
QUILT

CARRYING THE NOT-VERY-ROMANTIC name of Pickle Dish, this cheery pattern is a variation of the single most popular quilt design of the twentieth century, Double Wedding Ring. Composed of interlocking circular shapes that cover the entire quilt, Double Wedding Ring seem to appeal to just about everyone. In fact, during the quilting revival of the 1930s such quilts were de riguer for any maker with a bit of experience. Although the patterns required the use of difficult-to-sew, curved shapes, they presented just enough of a challenge to the Depression era quilter to keep her mind off her husband's jobless state. In addition, the pattern did not require the purchase of new fabric; it could be made successfully with any small scraps that might be on hand.

This deceptively simple Double Wedding Ring pattern attracts and holds the eye with its subtle colorations and contrasting outlines set against a brilliant red field.

The origins of the Double Wedding Ring are surprisingly vague. Similar, interlocking circular designs appeared in other decorative arts (ceramic tile, for example) as early as the 1860s, and conventional wisdom held that a similar quilt pattern probably appeared soon after the Civil War. While this may well be true, nineteenth-century examples are rare and most Double Wedding Ring designs date after 1920. By the 1930s, one can speculate that the streamlining of everything from

motorcars to toasters must have encouraged quilters to abandon their linear geometry for these rolling curves. It is known that during that decade the pattern was widely disseminated through a phenomenon called the "Nancy Page Quilt Club," a syndicated newspaper column. In this popular feature, a mythical teacher chatted with a group of students about the quilt pattern of the week.

Most quilt patterns are known by a few different names but the ubiquitous Double Wedding Ring pattern has been called by a record number of thirty-eight. This particular version, Pickle Dish, is thought to have been inspired by the cut-glass dishes that were popular in the early twentieth century. It is very similar to a version called Indian Wedding Ring and to another called Pine Burr which was especially popular in the South between 1930 and 1940. At first glance it looks very different from conventional Wedding Ring patterning. Where are the distinctive rings set against a solid color background? A closer look reveals that here in Pickle Dish the quilter has simply accentuated different parts of the endless grid of interlocking circles on which the pattern is based.

Here the areas of overlap between the circles—rather than the circles themselves—have been made the focus of the viewer's eye. The quilter has chosen to fill in these areas of overlap so that they suddenly become petal shapes that seem to crisscross in a new pattern across the quilt. But look carefully and you can just make out the circles formed by any two sets of juxtaposed petals. The quilter has actually made it harder for us to do this by making each half of the circle a different color. Its almost as if she intended to hide this quilt's Wedding Ring origins. But the tiny rectangular pieces that make up each circle and the divided squares that mark each intersection are too familiar to mistake. It's Pickle Dish all right, executed in the usual pale Depression colors, but set against an unusually brilliant red background more typical of nineteenth-century quilts. It may not scream Double Wedding Ring, but its graphic, visual impact comes across loud and clear. If painter Frank Stella were ever to make a quilt it might look something like this. ✩

THE VICTORIAN CHRISTMAS QUILT

"I ALWAYS THOUGHT [my grandmother's] was the prettiest quilt I ever saw," wrote John Rice Irwin, author of *A People and Their Quilts.* "But the only time she ever used it was around Christmas time. She'd get it out a few days before Christmas and use it as a bedcover 'til around the first of the year; then she'd put it away for another year. She made it, I think, about the time she was married in the late 1890s."

Mr. Irwin might have been describing this very quilt—which was probably made in time to celebrate Christmas of 1893. It is so pretty that it's easy to imagine its owner wanting to spare it from heavy use, and so festive that, in spite of its summery, floral subject matter, it looks a lot like Christmas—a very Victorian Christmas—with white flower garlands in the parlor, a tree festooned with golden moons and stars, and sentimental ladies' handiwork gifts lurking among the colored paper. The quilt itself is, of course, a prime example of the latter. It is a veritable festival of the decorative techniques practiced by Victorian women, as well as a cornucopia of the genteel symbolism that characterized that gas-lit age.

In addition to its clear inscription, "Merry X Mas," the quilt contains a few other nods to the season, includ-

ing a rather nicely executed crown of thorns and a prominent rendition of a calla lily, since the Middle Ages a universal symbol of the Virgin Mary. The presence of a horseshoe and what appears to be a Pennsylvania Dutch hex sign remind us that the quilt was made during a gently superstitious era, while a whole catalogue of flowers provides the hidden meanings and innuendo necessary to any Victorian courtship. In the "language of flowers" spoken by everybody who was anybody, the red bud at the very bottom meant "pure and lovely" while the pansies were "for thoughts." The hearts sprinkled around the quilt suggest that this may have been the work of a prospective bride. The initials "J.A.T." are prominently displayed near the quilt's date. Was J.A.T. our blushing maker, or were those perhaps the initials of her intended?

We do know that this quiltmaker was an accomplished practicioner of the Victorian decorative arts, and a person with a clear, individual sense of design. She picked and chose among the traditional elements of the Crazy Quilt (popular in the 1870s and 1880s), selecting some and discarding others, to create exactly the quilt she envisioned. Gone are the crazy abstract shapes, pieced onto a basic square of muslin and connected with a web of decorative stitchery. This is a traditional, pieced block quilt—plain and simple—with appliqué work on top. There are seventy-two different blocks and because they are of varying shades of black, the boundaries of each is clearly apparent. Still, such a black background is a typical element of the Crazy Quilt, in which black satin and especially velvet played a major role. Also typical are the floral

This Victorian masterpiece of appliqué, in which flowers, stars, and moons seem to dance against the inky blackness of the midnight sky, adds a whimsical touch to the festive room.

decoration, Victorian symbolism, and complicated decorative embellishments.

Among the embellishments represented here are elaborate, three-dimensional flowers (as in the central motif) worked in metallic thread. Even more frequent are the hand-painted vignettes (looking almost like tiny moving pictures appearing out of the surrounding blackness), interspersed with sentimental renditions of birdies crooning on their branch and of course, more flowers. Perhaps our maker agreed with the lady quoted in *The Ohio Farmer* back in 1884, who wrote of her quilt-making: "I painted flowers on some of the blocks; they are much prettier than embroidery and not so much work." Such painting was also something of a fad. The ladies of the era delighted in using it to decorate screens, curtains, whatever came to hand.

Altogether, this charming and worthy Christmas offering must have delighted its recipient. Where would it have been displayed? On the parlor piano or hassock—the usual venues for the Victorian Crazy Quilt—or, for a special winter night or two, in the nursery. For what is Christmas without the image of sleeping children "nestled all snug in their beds"? ✩

THE
COXCOMB
& BIRDS
VARIATION
QUILT

THIS CHARMING QUILT, dating from about 1860, came with an old, crumpled note attached, bearing the inscription "Eda Barnes, Barnesville, Ohio." So few quilts can tell us anything at all about their genesis or subsequent history that we can't help wondering about the meaning of this tiny clue: Was Eda Barnes just another owner of the quilt, coming onto the scene long after it was made? Or was she the maker or one of her descendents?

Barnesville is a town of about five thousand residents in Belmont County, near the West Virginia border. It was founded in 1808 by James Barnes who came to Ohio from Baltimore County, Maryland. By the 1850s the town was a small metropolis boasting a post office, hotel, and a number of mills. Although the name Eda Barnes does not appear in the mid-nineteenth-century records kept by the local geneological society, the amateur historians of Barnesville did stumble across one Adda Barnes who lived in Barnesville about 1908 and was the organizer of a major quilt exhibition held there at that time. Perhaps this was our Eda with her name misspelled (although she would have been well along in years by 1908—or maybe her granddaughter who,

having grown up with beautiful quilts, wanted to share their wonders with the town at large. Whether Adda or Eda, the maker of this quilt was one interesting, independent woman. What is at first glance a standard, mid-century example made in the nine-block format to a pattern known as Coxcomb, is actually a whimsical, highly idiosyncratic masterpiece of American folk art.

The Coxcomb design itself is not particularly noteworthy. It was a popular flower, found in all mid-century seed catalogues and particularly beloved of Americans of Scottish descent for its similarity to the thistle, symbol of Scottish unity and pride. But none of the dozens of known Coxcomb quilt patterns include the strange, unidentifiable shape appliquéd at intervals in green with red accents on this quilt. What is it, exactly? A butterfly, a snail? Another plant? With all of its exacting little "teeth" it matches the ruffling on the coxcomb blossoms, so it seems to belong to the composition. It is also strategically positioned so that it balances the three-pronged shape formed by the coxcomb and its leaves.

Miss Barnes went off the reservation in several other interesting ways. While her eagle is the classic, well-proportioned American shape used in many of the decorative arts of the period, her other birds are more like creatures out of a Dr. Seuss book. An unidentified bird with an extravagantly feathered tail perches on a coxcomb leaf several times its size. Her peacocks are more conventional but they are also tiny—smaller than the swallows that sail above them all around the border— and with furled tails. Such incongruities of scale are familiar to anyone who knows American folk art (New England overmantel paintings teem with huge birds sitting on small branches and vice-versa), but are unusual in the quilt idiom. The spindly, flowery stems that grace all four sides of Miss Barnes' border are another unusual, folkish, overmantel touch.

Folk art painters were usually rural, untutored types who, having never seen any academic art, simply drew from their imaginations. It is unlikely that a Civil War-era resident of Barnesville, Ohio, could have been so cloistered, but it is possible that she was a well-brought up young lady who eschewed standard patterns in favor of her own unique hand-drafted designs. They are, after all, quite balanced, symmetrical, and skillfully executed. The appliqué and quilting is exquisite, as is the trapunto (stuffed work) that decorates the white areas of the quilt. Miss Barnes was obviously good at measuring as well. She organized the quilt so that when it is placed on a double bed its center just covers the top and its borders hang down exactly to the floor. We think we understand the multitalented Miss Barnes and we like her. Now, if we could only figure out what she was trying to tell us with those odd red and green snail-like shapes. ☆

Although this charming floral pattern was designed to be seen on a double bed, it would be equally effective on a table top or draped over a sofa back.

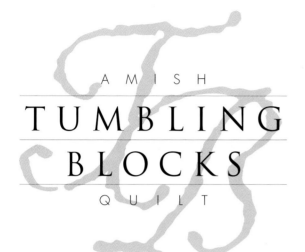

AMISH
TUMBLING
BLOCKS
QUILT

IT'S EASY TO SEE WHY this pattern is called Tumbling Blocks and why it is considered among the most successful illusionary quilt patterns of all time. Blink, and you will begin to doubt your own vision. The three-dimensional cubes will seem to turn into ribbons, undulating across the quilt. Blink again and the blocks are back, falling in a geometric waterfall that ends abruptly at the border. This quilt, made in 1935, is all about fooling the eye—and pleasing it at the same time. Thanks to the sophisticated color scheme chosen by its maker, an Amish quilter from La Grange County, Indiana, it is as beautiful as it is illusionary.

That aesthetic partnership is an old story. The concept of trompe l'oeil, or fooling the eye with the decoration of objects, goes back thousands of years. The Tumbling Blocks pattern itself has been traced to ancient tile work, and many such illusionary patterns pepper the art history of later Western civilization, turning up in the jewel tones of stained glass, the exquisite mosaic of cloisonée, and in the satiny inlaid patterns that pop out at the viewer from two-dimensional wooden tabletops and cupboard doors. This perennial fascination with optical effects also led, in 1817, to the invention of the kaleidoscope—a gizmo which, with a flick of the wrist, allows the geometric pattern at the end of a tube to change before your very eyes.

The illusion of movement, of change, in this Tum-

bling Blocks quilt is created by our own eyes which can register only one pattern at a time effectively. We may first see a series of cubes, perfectly shaded for perspective, one forming the border of the next. But if the eye keeps on looking, another pattern may suddenly predominate and we may see for example, a red ribbon snaking across the quilt, shaded as it bends away from us, brighter as it comes forward into the light. That ribbon can also be read obliquely from top left to bottom right, although now it is pale blue and red on a dark, receding background. The quilter has accomplished all of this with her choice of colors, which create shadow and perspective by means of cleverly juxtaposed light and dark tones.

The Indiana Amish were experts at this kind of optical balancing act, with a superb color sense unique among American quilters. Although generally more liberal than their

The architectonic lines of the Tumbling Blocks pattern provide an effective visual complement to the well-polished partitions of this wine cabinet.

brethren in Lancaster County, Pennsylvania, they continued to maintain a lifestyle purposefully separated from their "English" neighbors. Stressing modesty, spirituality, and functional plainness in all things, the Indiana Amish quilters were brought up in homes in which patterned linoleum and wallpaper and popular magazines were less common. Their color sense remained individualistic and highly developed. Unlike the Lancaster Amish, the Amish of Ohio and Indiana borrowed freely from the pattern stocks of their neighbors, producing exceptional, distinctly Amish, renditions of popular patterns like Tumbling Blocks and Ocean Waves.

Tumbling Blocks, also known as Stair Steps and Illusion, was made by quilters of many stripes. Constructed in an allover pattern of repeating shapes (as opposed to being composed of blocks that form the pattern), it turned up in silk in the Victorian Crazy Quilts, appeared in varied printed calicoes throughout the late-nineteenth and early-twentieth centuries, and was common to most areas of the country, including the South where it was known as Baby Blocks.

But perhaps the Amish aesthetic best suits this memorable, changeable pattern. Working most often in plain cotton, Amish makers brought to Tumbling Blocks a purity, simplicity, and skill that intensifies its illusionary effect: The flawless, straight lines of the quilting are eminently suited to the other patterning, not distracting from the illusion, but leading the eye along linear paths. Plain, non-figural fabrics in rich, saturated colors heighten the contrast of dark and light, the play of positive and negative space on which the illusion is based. While we're being dazzled by our quiltmaker's aesthetic choices, we should not overlook her unquestionable skill, showcased by the endless diamond shapes that make up the pattern: To make them the fabric must be cut on the bias. It may stretch more easily than fabric cut along the grain and play potential havoc with careful measurements. ✩

THE "SWEET WINGS" QUILT

TEN YEARS AGO QUILT ARTIST Karen Felicity Berkenfeld decided not to make any more quilts. A New York City resident who worked in wool, using traditional quilt construction and non-traditional subject matter, she intended to forsake the medium in favor of another love, printmaking. It didn't last. Within weeks her paper supply was gathering dust and Berkenfeld, a collector of vintage fabric printing blocks, was experimenting with new ways to print on fabric. Inevitably, her unique printed textiles began to find their way into quilts. "The quilt is my medium," Berkenfeld soon realized. "People were constantly saying, 'Why don't you just print on paper?' But there is something about cutting pieces apart and sewing them into something else that to me is important and enjoyable."

Once back among the ranks of quiltmakers, Berkenfeld was not at all sorry that she strayed—however briefly—from the fold. Because in doing so, she came upon what has now become her signature style. Calling herself a textile printer and quiltmaker, Berkenfeld incorporates into her quilts fabrics that are themselves works of art. Using varied processes like collagraph, linoleum cut, monoprint, and etching, Berkenfeld creates unusual artistic effects on fabric—from soft and painterly to hard edged—and

As arresting as any painting, but with a textural richness no painted canvas can match, Karen Felicity Berkenfeld's Sweet Wings *is the perfect spot of color in this monochromatic interior.*

uses these new, irreplaceable textiles to make her quilts. So important to her oeuvre is the hand-printed fabric that she uses it nearly exclusively; only about twenty-five percent of the fabric in her quilts is storebought.

Such quiltmaking is a labor intensive, multiprocess endeavor, but it is a natural part of a life that, from the very beginning, has been full of the joy of making things. Born into a family of artists and artistic laypeople, Berkenfeld remembers growing up surrounded by aesthetically sensitive people who valued good craftsmanship, and being constantly encouraged by them to create out of fabric and wood. Fabric quickly became her first love

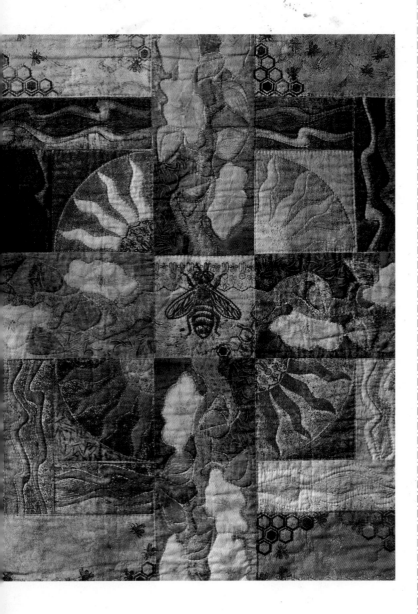

and this attraction, along with her growing collection of antique quilts and folk art, finally pushed her in the direction of quiltmaking. As quilters have done for hundreds of years, Berkenfeld began to draw on the sources of inspiration in her own life.

In *Sweet Wings* for example, Berkenfeld remembers a beloved sister, her constant childhood companion, who died at a young age over twenty years ago. A mutual friend had engraved her headstone with the first lines of a Japanese haiku, "One fallen flower, returning to the branch," but try as she might, Berkenfeld had never succeeded in locating the last line. Deciding to finish the poem herself, she incorporated into it her own persona of beekeeper (a hobby she indulges at a house in upstate New York) and completed the haiku with the quilt's title, "Sweet wings to the hive." Her quilt's imagery, which includes the bee motif, gently Japonesque flowers, and the rising sun, are all appropriate to Berkenfeld's evocation of love, loss, and the continuation of life.

To create the rich textural mélange that forms the background to this imagery, Berkenfeld turned to the process of collagraph—literally, printmaking with collage. She layered a cardboard "printing plate" with materials like lace, coffee grounds, and tea leaves, then glued her texture-producing flotsam in place, inked her "plate," and ran off-white cotton fabric through the printing press. The ink was squeezed into the fabric in the pattern created by her collage. She created the central bee and honeycomb motifs with linoleum cuts and rubber-stamped other hovering bees. Batting and backing were stitched into place, and the final product was hand-quilted around the edges of the images. Although the quilting is not central to the visual impact of *Sweet Wings*, Berkenfeld is not coy about her art's identity. "I want it to be seen as a quilt," she says firmly. "It is a thing itself—not a picture of a thing." ☆

THE
CROSSED
LEAVES
APPLIQUÉ
QUILT

THINK OF THIS QUILT as a rich dessert with layers of hidden delights beneath its whipped cream surface. The first layer of pattern is the most obvious one— a charming allover design of crossed flowering branches appliquéd onto an off-white background. But a closer look at that background reveals the presence of a whole other decorative universe—a hidden garden of exquisite, white-on-white floral patterns executed in three-dimensional stuffed work, or trapunto. Look even closer: Those patterns rise up out of painstaking stippling—millions of tiny stitches creating an allover textured ground—adding yet another layer of richness and depth. It's a tour de force of quilting quite different from bold geometric patterning. This quilt is more like an eighteenth-century French writing table on which ormolu is framed by fruitwood inlay, or a great Meissen platter in which painted flowers are cradled by molded patterns. For hundreds of years these amalgams of pattern and texture have proved greater than the sum of their parts.

Mid-nineteenth-century America was the era of sophisticated textural integration in quilting. During these decades, appliqué and piecework joined stuffed work and stippling on the quilt top—equal partners in a unique aesthetic enterprise. Such quilts were not for beginners, but were long-term, labor-intensive operations in which

every skill counted: The appliqué pattern had to be well chosen, then carefully cut and stitched; the background stippling had to be patiently built up of countless tiny stitches. Appliqué and piecework patterns might have been obtained from a neighbor or the *Godey's Lady's Book*, but designs for stuffed work were obtained in a less direct way, cribbed from wallpaper, textiles, or other decorative objects, then copied and rearranged to fit the space available and complement the surrounding appliqué.

Then one had to get down to the stuffing itself. This is a venerable skill dating back to the fourteenth century. The best known examples however, were made in eighteenth-century Europe, where the work was known as Marseilles quilting. Ladies' fashions of the period called for a split overskirt that left a central panel exposed from waist to toe. These prominent expanses of petticoat were decorated in the following manner: A loosely woven backing was paired with another piece of fabric; then, using fine stitching, decorative designs (often floral) were outlined on the top piece, effectively quilting the

two together. Using a bodkin (or blunt needle), yarn, cotton, or cording was stuffed through the backing and into the channels left by the stitching. When the desired fullness had been obtained, these openings were sewn closed. Some descriptions of the process suggest that the gauzy backing was then cut away and replaced by a stronger backing. Others note that the openings made by the bodkin and its trail of cording could be effectively shrunk back to proper size after the first washing.

The term "Marseilles quilting" is rarely used in quilt circles. Instead, "trapunto," an Italian word meaning "quilt" and the more evocative "stuffed work" are the terms of choice. The term "Matalese" is currently used to describe a modern, less elaborate version of the same technique. In the nineteenth century, when stuffed work was paired with stippling (as in this example), embroidery, and candlewicking (another three-dimensional technique), the finished quilt or coverlet was sometimes identified as "white work."

Our nineteenth-century quilter is known to have lived in Ohio. Other than that, she has left us only her initials, MSO, signed in the quilting, and the year, 1853. Whoever she was, she paired Fifth Avenue with the Village Green. Her floral appliqué is a sprigged red calico with a plain green for the leaves. The pattern is simple and probably of German derivation. With its graphic, generic blossoms it could have come off a fraktur in a Pennsylvania Dutch household. Then, MSO took quite a different route for her stuffed work. Here,

Plain and understated when viewed at a distance, this quilt is actually an elegant, intricate masterpiece of appliqué, stuffed work, and stippling.

sophisticated urns and baskets hold stylized blooms and foliage in graceful attitudes—a white-on-white rendition of imported European wallpaper that might have hung in a Fifth Avenue drawing room. It's rather a tease, really, with its layer of simplicity hiding the glories underneath. No wonder this quilt has made it down to us some one hundred forty years later. It's too beautiful to use. In fact, it looks good enough to eat. ✧

EARLY
CALICO &
CHINTZ
QUILT

THE MAKER OF THIS ca. 1840s quilt was clearly fascinated by the possibilities of fabric—its color, its pattern, its ability to juxtapose and combine into something effective and beautiful. In particular, she seems to be asking us to think about calico and chintz and the interesting aesthetic differences between these two ubiquitous mid-nineteenth-century fabrics.

At the time this quilt was made, calico and chintz were still spoken of interchangeably, referring to any printed cotton fabric. In fact, the two are quite different from each other, and by about 1850, the general public had sorted them out. Chintz is a large-figured cotton, usually glazed, usually printed in some kind of floral pattern, and was (and continues to be) used mainly as furnishing (upholstery) fabric. The word comes from a transliteration of a Hindi word meaning "variegated" and was first seen in print, spelled "chints," about 1614. The word "calico" comes from its birthplace, the city of Calicut on India's western coast, one of that country's most important cotton weaving centers. On these shores after about 1850, the term calico was used exclusively to refer to plain-weave cotton dress goods printed with small motifs, both floral and abstract.

In the emotional lexicon of most Americans, each of these fabrics holds a very different place. Chintz is fancy,

foreign, bringing to mind images of upscale decorating—Park Avenue drawing rooms with tasseled curtains puddling on the floor. During the entire nineteenth century, chintz remained the more expensive choice and so appears in relatively fewer quilts. Calico, on the other hand, has always been the very fabric of American populist history. It was the stuff that Ma and the girls always bought at the general store, the stuff of work dresses and aprons, the curtains at the window of the little house on the prairie. Quiltwise, it has always been, hands-down, the most popular choice.

However different these two fabrics seem to us, to late-seventeenth-century European textile makers they were both cotton, and that's all they needed to know. Imported cottons were new on the market and a huge threat to the monopolies long enjoyed by the silk and woolen weavers of Europe. The importation and manufacture of chintz and calico were banned there and, naturally, this shortage immediately made them very fashionable indeed. Intensive smuggling ensued and in England, makers found their way around the problem by printing on a fabric called fustian (a linen/cotton blend). By the 1820s the ban had been lifted and the focus had shifted from Europe to America where English makers were dumping their cotton goods at lower prices in an effort to squelch development of local industry here. It didn't work. Although English cottons continued to be imported here until about 1850 (and so may have found their way into this very quilt), by the 1840s American textile mills

Richly figured chintz squares help make this quilt look very much at home in a drawing room setting, where such fabrics have long been traditional choices for upholstery and curtains.

were also running full blast. Although fabric selection was quite extensive all over, the prices were better near the point of manufacture. In 1841 the same cotton fabric that sold for 2½ cents a yard in Hartford, Connecticut, cost a whopping 25 cents a yard faraway in Iowa.

Our quilter took full advantage of the fabric selection in her area—in both chintz and calico. Her choices were typical of early nineteenth-century New England makers who tended to use richly colored, figural textiles to create dark, densely patterned bedcovers. (Their Southern counterparts veered more toward bright chintz appliqué on snowy white.) She was also clearly aware of the effectiveness of playing different types of fabric off each other. She used a rather fabulous burnt orange, milk chocolate, and white chintz for setting squares (single fabric patches designed to show off the patchwork between them), but made the chintz, not the calico patchwork, the focal point. (The tiny, dark, patterned calicoes are a perfect contrast though, effectively showcasing the chintz's bold appeal.) Around this wide center area, she used two other pieced calico patterns, each made up of a zippy "lead" fabric surrounded by darker, more retiring materials. These patterns also vary the geometry of the quilt—one features triangles, the other diamonds—but even with all their complicated piecework they remain supporting players to the bright squares of eye catching chintz, the lead actors in this quilting drama. ✩

"VACATION VIGNETTES"

"I PAINT WITH FABRIC," says Michigan quilt artist Sue Holdaway-Heys. "I start with broad, large pieces and build up my composition with smaller pieces, layering as I go, using lots of different materials, zigzagging them in with matching thread. I always work upright—like any other painter," she adds. "Then I can step back from what I'm doing and see how it will 'read' when it is finished and hanging on the wall."

It's a fascinating image—an artist facing her easel, wielding bits of fabric like a paintbrush—placing one here, then there, then going back to the well of prepared strips and squares, like a painter dipping into the pigments on a loaded palette, bringing color and shape into being before our very eyes. It's not what we usually imagine when we think of quiltmaking, but for Holdaway-Heys, a painterly use of fabric seems almost inevitable. Her life has led her inexorably to her current artistic incarnation: "I've been an artist forever," she says. "Even when I was a child I knew that this is what I would do—there was never any doubt. First I got a BA in art education—I taught high school art for a number of years. I also became a painter and a fiber artist, weaving on a big double-beam floor loom. The change to painter/quiltmaker was originally a matter of practicality. Pregnant with her first child, Holdaway-Heys "simply couldn't bend over the loom anymore. So I thought, 'what can I do instead?' and I

Sue Holdaway-Heys' ocean-blue and sunshine yellow evocation of family holidays by the sea is the perfect complement to the light-filled setting of this indoor swimming pool.

decided to take a quilting class. I learned all the basics—sewing, appliqué, and off I went."

Like many contemporary quilt artists, Holdaway-Heys started out by making traditional quilts but quickly decided that her talents lay elsewhere. "By 1981 all the old patterns were out the window," she remembers. "I began 'painting with fabric,' interpreting subjects from my own life—my perennial garden, my family, the natural world around me." Holdaway-Heys had found her niche. When she went back to school (at the age of forty) to get her MFA, it was as a quiltmaker, although her advisors expressed surprised at her choice, wondering why she insisted on working in fabric rather than in paint. This in turn surprised Holdaway-Heys. The tactile qualities of her medium were so clearly appealing.

This appeal is evident in *Vacation Vignettes*, which Holdaway-Heys made as "a kind of memory quilt" after a family vacation at Hilton Head. Using photos of her children as a reference point, the artist painted their images onto fabric, then made these paintings focal points in a rich mélange of other textiles—cutting and piecing, then quilting to add another layer of texture. Evocations of sun and cool water were created with a range of pale yellows and deep blues. The placement of every strip and every square of fabric is precise and important. Some seem to frame the images, while others seem placed for maximum textural and visual impact. The complicated, virtuoso quilting is an important decorative element in itself and adds to our awareness that what we are seeing is indeed fabric and not a flat layer of paint.

THE "LAKEVIEW" QUILT

"I AM AN ARTIST who chooses to work in the quilt medium," says Holdaway-Heys. In *Lakeview* I am drawing with my needle." This landscape in fabric possesses the soft, atmospheric qualities of an American Luminist painting. The composition too is classic, reminiscent of a Hudson River landscape (though the image is actually of a Michigan lake) with a near and middle distance leading the eye away to an infinity of pink-tinged hills. The sky and water reflect each other's gentle grayness. Instead of painterly brushstrokes, we have quilting in various organic patterns that give textures to the land, water, and foliage. This quilt begins with the dyeing of fabric in melting shades and the layering onto a base material of hundreds of pieces of fabric that dissolve into one another, the edges softened with subtly colored thread.

While Holdaway-Heys's elaborate quilting, use of printed fabrics, and inclusion of block forms all seem to be a nod to quilting's past, there is nothing old-fashioned about her work. Closer in spirit to Mondrian or Rauschenberg than Nine-Patch or Tumbling Blocks, it reflects the artist's interests in contemporary art of all kinds. "I identify with what our ancestors did," says Holdaway-Heys. "But I don't want to make a Lone Star quilt anymore. I've done that. In fact it's been done eight thousand times. I want to do quilts in my own style, with my own patterns. My quiltmaking is not a hobby. It's my life." ✦

Sue Holdaway-Heys' Lakeview *is as evocative an American landscape as any painting, but as a quilt, is also a beautifully made decorative object.*

THE BOTANICAL APPLIQUÉ

MID-NINETEENTH-CENTURY American women were serious about flowers. Scores of magazines and books devoted to landscape design, gardening, and the language of flowers stressed the importance of these interests to the elevation of taste, purity, religion—even good parenting. Andrew Jackson Downing, that gentlemanly advocate of home beautification, advised "the ladies of the household" to cultivate flower gardens for such an activity would be "conducive to their own health, and to the beauty and interest of our homes." *Godey's Lady's Book* got on the bandwagon, publishing elaborate plans for gardens and other articles of a botanical nature. Interest in botanizing (studying and collecting botanical specimens) was reaching epidemic proportions. "Every Victorian young lady it seemed," wrote Lynn Barber in *The Heyday of Natural History*, "could reel off the names of twenty different kinds of ferns or fungus." Gamboling in the woods and fields in search of interesting specimens was considered a healthful activity, appropriately chaste and useful, leading to the making of desirable ornaments like wax flowers, feather flowers, flower paintings, floral scrapbooks, and, of course, floral quilts.

Flowers were not only uplifting, they were important symbolic objects useful both to communication and the contemplation of the human condition. The wilting bloom was the universal Victorian symbol of the transitory nature of life, while particular flowers were officially delegated to represent specific sentiments or ideas, composing an unofficial language that fascinated and titilated repressive Victorian society. A young man could for example, present a cowslip to a young lady and announce "you are my divinity," without uttering a word. Flower dictionaries became popular gifts between young women, who would spend hours together giddily translating exactly what that last floral tribute really meant.

Decoding the flowers "CS" appliquéd on this quilt in 1851, we could posit an interesting love story indeed. The maker's inclusion of petunias exhorts someone to "never despair" while the red-and-yellow variegated tulip croons "beautiful eyes." More interesting still, that morning glory stands for "affectation." We'll never know exactly what CS was trying to say, but we can guess that in making this quilt, she was concentrating more on design than botany. The shapes of her flowers probably came down to her from her mother or the mother of a neighbor—American simplifications of European designs that originated centuries earlier in China. Hers are not careful records made after a botanizing field trip. They are charming, improbable floral concoctions in which blossoms of several colors bloom from the same stalk and the accompanying leaves seem to have been chosen for their design value rather than for their botanical correctness.

Some of CS's other decisions are more of a mystery. Although, with its careful presentation of individual floral designs this quilt fits technically into the category of sampler, most samplers were constructed in blocks, each containing one featured pattern. CS has chosen to appliqué her quilt top as a whole. Even more curious, she's not big on symmetry, presenting two lines with five flower images each, one with only four, and another in which the fifth "flower" is a vignette of a little house, turned on its side and next to some pine trees. Her initials (featuring only one period, not two) and the date are oddly placed up near the top, prominently displayed, yet appear to be almost an afterthought. What could she have been thinking?

Perhaps she was wiser than we think. The inclusion of that little sideways house is a real attention grabber— practically guaranteeing that we will look hard at the rest of the quilt, trying to figure out what the house is doing there. She also may have borrowed for her own purposes, that old tradition of all good Christian quilters, intentionally making one mistake to acknowledge that only God can make something perfect. Her off-kilter design is another fortuitous move, making us examine every one of her odd, hybrid cuttings— allowing us to accept nothing at face value. Perhaps she started casually one day with one flower, admired each new addition as she worked, and finally ended up with a quilt she was proud enough to sign. How beautiful it must have been in 1851 when its now faded yellow green was a rich, deep, foresty shade. How beautiful it is still. ☆

This charming Victorian appliquéd quilt brings nature indoors and adds warmth to the living room in early spring.

PINK
DOGWOOD
IN BASKETS
QUILT

DURING THE COLONIAL REVIVAL of the early twentieth century, designers of all stripes looked to early American sources for their inspiration. In turn, American women took to their needles to produce quilts appropriate to a Colonial interior. But as our grandmothers diligently reproduced red and green stars and calico patchwork, many wished for a new kind of quilt pattern—one that would reconcile the traditions of the nineteenth century with a more contemporary look. The world around them was changing so quickly. Hemlines were rising, the phonograph was blaring, Lindberg was flying the Atlantic in a silver plane, and Hollywood was creating a longing for glamour and beauty. Into this new reality came the quilt designer Marie Daugherty Webster (1859–1956)—the answer to the quilting industry's prayers. Her patterns were modern and yet sufficiently traditional, and so alluring, so feminine, so breathtakingly beautiful, that they literally pulled quilt design into the twentieth century.

She was born Marie Daugherty in Wabash, Indiana, but in 1884 when she married George Webster she became a resident of the neighboring town of Marion. There, Marie's sophisticated quilt designs so impressed her friends and relations that they begged her to submit them to that reigning oracle of American womankind, the

Ladies' Home Journal. Webster's first designs appeared in that magazine in 1911. By 1912 she was the new national quilt authority, and had been given the job as needlecraft editor at the magazine—a position she held until 1917. During this time she was also contracted by Doubleday to write the first full-length book on quilts. *Quilts: Their Story and How to Make Them*, published in 1915 and a huge success, traced the history of quiltmaking, provided designs suitable for quilting and a long list of traditional pattern names. It also promoted Webster's own particular aesthetic, which favored appliqué over piecing, solid pastel colors, and realistic floral designs that were arranged to achieve maximum effect when the quilt was spread out, in all of its pastel glory, over its owner's bed.

Nineteenth-century floral quilt designs were so stylized that simple triangles and other geometric shapes had been all a quilter needed to master. Webster's irises and roses, sunflowers and dogwood blossoms were another matter. They were challenging in their complexity, and quilters quickly found that detailed patterns and kits were a big help. While still at *Ladies' Home Journal* Webster started an extremely successful mail-order business, selling

Pink Dogwood in Baskets is typical of the glamorous, pastel floral quilts designed by Marie Webster in the 1920s and 30s.

new, eye-catching designs to her customers every year —some based on traditional patterns but most original. The company offered quilt kits at $12, basted quilt tops at $37.50, and completely finished examples at a rather reasonable $50. Buying a finished version of course, would save the trouble of doing all of the work oneself or even of employing, as many early-twentieth-century quilters did, a professional quilter to add the final layer of ornament.

Marie Webster became the single most frequently copied quilt designer of the early twentieth century. Her patterns were adapted and borrowed by newspapers around the country for their quilt columns, and also by Stearns & Foster—the Cincinnati company that printed patterns inside their roles of Mountain Mist cotton batting. Webster, and the other designers from which these companies "borrowed" (including Rose Kretsinger and Anne Orr), were never credited, despite the fact that they were almost singlehandedly responsible for reviving quiltmaking as a twentieth-century pursuit. It was these women who set the stage for Stearns & Foster's success and led the company to publish the 1933 pamphlet "The Romance of the Quilt: Making Sales," which trumpeted that "quilt making is highly profitable to any and every merchant who will promote it."

Marie Webster's success was guaranteed by patterns like this one—Pink Dogwood in Baskets, offered in *Ladies' Home Journal* in 1927. It is typical of her style in that it is a floral pattern made with solid-color fabrics in melting pastel colors used as in nature (pink blossoms, green leaves), set against a paler background. The elaborate border looks wonderful hanging off the end of the bed. The flowers are slightly stylized—but would still be identifiable by any horticulturalist. The magazine audience of 1927 must have gasped with pleasure and marveled at Webster's seemingly unending fund of inspiration when they saw this pattern. It was a gift that the lady had, and we are glad that she shared it with the world. ✩

CALICO
BLAZING STAR
QUILT

ONE OF THE MOST INTRIGUING aspects of studying antique American quilts is seeing which of the hundreds of elements of traditional quiltmaking each maker chose to incorporate into her unique and beautiful finished product. Sometimes it was only the choice of color or fabric that made this magic—no two Double Wedding Ring quilts are exactly the same, for example. But in the case of this calico and chintz masterpiece, ca. 1860, the quilter made many unusual choices.

The center motif of this quilt is known as the Blazing Star—an eight-pointed star that, with the addition of surrounding layers, seems to be giving off a vaporous, burning light. It was a common enough nineteenth-century design, often formed as this one was, of small diamond-shaped sections of small patterned fabrics. However, most blazing stars appear in groups, or in tandem with some other pattern, and the few that appear solo almost never behave as this one does. Look carefully and notice that after about layer six, this eight-pointed star suddenly becomes an octagon, that gets increasingly larger until it is no longer just a star, but a major event—a central medallion of majestic proportions.

By 1860 the central medallion was no longer quilting's most fashionable motif. The darling of appliqué quilts of the 1820s, it had long since given way to

mid-nineteenth-century America's penchant for cunning designs in patchwork executed in squares. This maker, however, managed to have her cake and eat it too. Her central medallion is a festival of complicated patchwork —sixteen different layers of pieced triangles, executed in over a dozen fabrics. As a tour de force of piecing it is so intricate, so carefully constructed—with its alternating bands of dark and light and its purposeful juxtaposition of color and scale—that sixteen layers is quite enough. We feel that if it had been allowed to continue out to the edges of the quilt that we might go blind looking at it.

Our quilter seems to have realized this and her solution was to employ another nearly passé technique. By 1860 the use of a whole-cloth chintz border was out of style. Indeed, its presence almost always signals a quilt from the first half of the century, when it was often used to unify quilts containing mix-and-match patches of calico and chintz. Our maker apparently didn't care about any of that. She seemed somehow to know that a bold, large-scale field of highly polished chintz would be the perfect foil for her finicky little calico diamonds—literally forcing our eye to acknowledge the complicated perfection of the central patchwork, even as it provides the eye with a place to rest. Did she happen to lay down her pieced octagon on an open bolt of chintz upholstery fabric destined for the parlor chairs and glancing down, shout, "Eureka!"?

Certainly the use of this particular chintz effectively balances any vestiges of old-fashionedness. It is an entirely sophisticated fabric, à la mode, wonderfully and completely Victorian (read: modern), apparently just off the boat from Kensington High Street. In fact, it may have been made at any one of a dozen New England mills. By 1860 American manufacturers were able to knock off such patterns within two to three weeks of their appearence on the shelves of European shops. To accomplish such speedy transatlantic copycatting, textile companies must have paid spies to snoop around fabric emporiums in Paris, Vienna, and London, pretending to be rich Bostonians planning new spring wardrobes. These imposters would then hand over their precious samples to accomplices who would board the fastest steamships and finally arrive, panting, with the booty, at the design departments at New England mills.

But however flashy this richly hued, large-scale chintz background, it is still just that—a background. It does not overwhelm the central motif but seems almost to recede to neutral, letting us enjoy the calico octagon in all its intricate glory. Besides, the strong graphic lines of this star-within-an-octagon-within-a-square can hold their own against any invasion of paisley or cabbage roses. Blink and you can see a painting by Kenneth Noland transformed into flowery fabric by some naughty performance artist. Except that this particular performance artist probably voted for Abraham Lincoln. ✩

Dark and rich like a Persian rug, this pieced, chintz-bordered quilt looks wonderful folded or draped, then unfurls to reveal a stunning central star.

THE
FLOUR
SACK
QUILT

RECYCLING IS A PUBLIC ACT in the late twentieth century, a communal task facilitated by burly truckers and white-coated functionaries who swirl melted plastic in antiseptic vats. But closer to our century's beginnings, the rescue and reuse of serviceable discards was a very personal quest—pursued by American housewives with a fervor today's throwaway society may find difficult to understand. Quilting itself was often part of this personal recycling, incorporating as it did the worn bits and pieces of family wardrobes. But when times were hardest and even those poor fragments were unavailable, the creative use of commerical packaging material could fill the gap. Fifty years ago flour, salt, tobacco, sugar, potatoes, fertilizer, even dog food, still came in fabric sacks. The material was rough but serviceable and, best of all, it was free when you bought the product it encased.

Plain, coarsely woven cotton muslin packaging bags were first produced in the mid-nineteenth century and by the early-twentieth century, were being used by thrifty women for the production of everything from aprons to underdrawers. In Harper Lee's Southern classic, *To Kill a Mockingbird*, the author invokes the poverty of her setting by referring to "the floursack skirted first grade." Some housewives proclaimed the humble sack-cloth to be better quality than many of the dress goods produced later,

but such stout defense may have covered feelings of shame. Anxious to override these feelings and promote sales, millers' and other trade associations provided handy instructions for the removal of the pesky trademarks. (However, at least one woman who used flour sacks to make her husband's underdrawers decided to leave the trademark on: It proclaimed "Self Rising.") When, in the 1930s, paper bag companies began to encroach on their territory, cloth bag manufacturers fought back with ever more tempting fabric offerings— floral print bags, catchy geometric patterns, and stick-on, easy-to-remove trademarks. All to no avail: By 1950 the days of fabric packaging were over.

Quilters had long been accustomed to utilizing sacking. In the second half of the nineteenth century, it was a popular base for Log Cabin and Crazy Quilt patterns. Blocks of such throwaway muslin would be cut and then covered with the appropriate small pieces, before being sewn together to form the quilt. Sacking was also a popular choice to back quilts of other patterns. In 1899 one reader wrote to *Progressive Farmer* magazine that six flour sacks would do to line a medium-sized quilt. But a few decades later, particularly in times of economic depression, such sacks began to turn up as pieces of the quilt top itself, sometimes in the form of recycled pieces cut from old feed sack aprons or housedresses, but often in the form of new sacking as well.

The sacks would be rescued from the trash pile and bleached to free them from printed trademarks (if this

Made entirely of fabric recycled from feed and other sacking, this ca. 1910 quilt is a true piece of Americana, as well as a sophisticated, rather minimalist work of art.

failed, one could always cut around the printed area), dyed, and cut to fit the pattern under construction. Such salvage became so common that during the 1930s, the Tennessee State Fair set up a special category for articles (including quilts) made out of recycled cotton sacks. When making rough and ready utility quilts not destined for any fair, some quilters wouldn't even bother to remove the labels, and later when floral and other printed bags became available, all one had to do was stock up on the right kind of sugar or fertilizer and then plan one's pattern accordingly. The thriftiest quilters even salvaged the string that closed the tops of the bags—in a pinch it made decent quilting thread.

Looking at this humorous example, a keen eye can make out the brand names that bleaching couldn't quite remove. Their shadow presence seems somehow appropriate for this quilt of no pretensions. This is no fancy Double Wedding Ring or Grandma's Flower Garden of sacking carefully dyed to make it look like store-bought fabric. Only the cotton strips appliquéd onto the plain feed sacks have been colored blue, and their charm is in their shape—not their color. With just an economic line here and there (look at the udders, for example) the quilter has suggested a cow with quite a personality. Made in Bowling Green, Kentucky, about 1910, it may well have been made for a child's bedroom. Did the lucky recipient mind that his quilt had come largely from the grocery store, or did he realize its sly charm? ✬

SAVANNAH STAR

THE OWNER OF THIS DRAMATIC quilt calls its pattern Savannah Star, but she is well aware that other quilt aficionados might disagree. They might refer to its eight-pointed, diamond-centered sparkler as an Ohio Star. And they'd all be right. It's all part of the legend of the star—the most beloved and frequently used motif in all of American quilting—and also one of the most confusing. At least one hundred quilt patterns incorporate this familiar image, bearing names that change from state to state, region to region, decade to decade. A pattern called the Texas Star in the West is referred to by Pennsylvanians as the Star of Bethlehem, while folks in the middle of the country know the same design as the Star of the East. Even in the same place, all it takes is one, often subtle, alteration in shape or size to change one star pattern into another—with yet another name.

But, why so many stars in the first place? It's an American natural: Start with the flag—there is no more patriotic, star-studded symbol—and consider how many quilt patterns are rooted in love of country. There was also the eighteenth- and nineteenth-century dependence on celestial navigation, not to mention the star's important role in the New Testament. No wonder this versatile motif appeared so frequently in all kinds of nineteenth-century folk art. Perhaps because of the patriotic connection, twenty-three states lend their names to star patterns —everything from the Kansas Star to the Michigan Star can be found in pattern books. Some stars take their names from their distinctive shape—the Feathered Star, the Broken Star—while others simply celebrate "star-i-ness" with names like Blazing Star, Radiant Star, and Morning Star. One of the most popular, a star made up of diamond shapes, is named for the LeMoyne brothers, the family that founded New Orleans in 1718. Just to confuse things, the LeMoyne Star is also known as the Lemon Star.

A single, central star pattern is often known as a Lone Star. This motif gained currency at about the same time as the Republic of Texas was founded, hence The Lone Star

As American as apple pie, this star pattern is executed in the classic, international colors of toile de Jouy *and Chinese porcelain—a fail-safe decorative addition to any interior.*

State. While popular, this pattern has fallen victim to one of the many untraceable superstitions connected with quilting: For some reason old-timers feared that a Lone Star quilt made without a secondary pattern surrounding its center motif would bring bad luck to its maker. Nevertheless, many quilters lived dangerously, loving the dramatic appearance of a single spreading star, which could be made to look impressive even when constructed with tiny bits of mismatched fabric. Although many star patterns are well suited to piecing with scraps, connecting so many right angles is a tricky business. Because of a star's construction, one wrong-sized piece will cause the whole star to pucker and compel its maker to start all over again.

The skilled needleworker who put together this example clearly had no such problems—and an eye for the dramatic to boot. A reverse, white-on-indigo blue combination was relatively rare in 1875. But after all, that is how stars appear in nature, a bright white glittering against a dark "sky." Here, a single indigo blue calico makes up the sky, while the stars, with their eight-sided points and diamond centers, seem to shine right in our eyes. Look away, and look at the pattern from another point of view: These are rather linear stars that, positioned as they are, are allowed to form a grid across the surface of the quilt. It's a clean, modern look, yet as traditional as they come—a combination that only the greatest quilts can boast. This one can also boast some age: Held up to the light, it shows a cotton interlining speckled with seeds. Although by 1875 Eli Whitney's cotton gin had long mechanized the seed removal process, throughout the nineteenth century quilters could still choose batting of varying quality—with fewer or more errant seeds. To the list of attributes already assigned to our patriotic, skillful maker we now add thrift. ✡

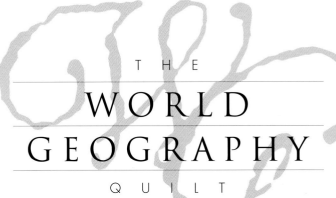

THE
WORLD
GEOGRAPHY
QUILT

BERTHA LOMAX FROE and Dorothy Lomax of Virginia were sisters—teachers with advanced degrees in education. They were also wonderful quilters. During the 1940s, apparently inspired by the images they saw monthly in *National Geographic* magazine (Dorothy had been subcribing since 1918), they pieced and appliquéd this around-the-world quilt. It's a wonderful object, and an important example of the long, fruitful tradition of quilting among African-Americans.

Quilting was not a traditional African activity but African-Americans quickly learned its ways, passing down their skills from generation to generation, often becoming extremely proficient. Slaves made many beautiful quilts for their masters and also supplemented meager livings by selling quilts outside their own plantations. Before and after the Civil War, African-Americans of all economic strata and geographic locations created quilts as diverse as the population itself. Following the same patterns and techniques as other American women, they created everything from elegant appliqués and pictorial quilts, to crazies and rough patchwork.

The whimsical vignettes that make up this travelogue of a quilt effortlessly coalesce into a powerful melange of pattern and color.

The question of whether African-American quilts are somehow distinguishable from others has been widely debated and remains unanswered. Some researchers point to a series of recognizable "African-American" characteristics including the dominance of stripes and the use of bright, highly contrasting colors, large design elements, offset designs and multiple patterning. Others point to certain stitch lengths and the use of assymetrical lines as common to "real" African-American quilts. These experts explain that the many African American made quilts that do not exhibit these particular traits are only copies of Caucasian designs and do not represent the true African-American vision. Other quilt specialists disagree, saying that because quilting was never an indigenous African activity, there is no "African" style that could have been carried over to African-American quiltmaking and that such pigeon-holing is a fruitless exercise.

Looking at this fascinating quilt we hardly care who wins the argument. Its composition of equally-sized pictorial blocks is uncommon—most pictorial quilts feature one large central motif surrounded by a border. The Lomax sisters seem to have borrowed the layout of an album quilt, and then filled their album with pictures of their imaginary travels. True, there is a large, featured central area—a sort of Eastern pastiche with Mt. Fuji and the Taj Mahal surrounded by various Japanese characters. Then suddenly we notice the little boy flying a very American-looking kite. He's standing quite near the lady in the kimono. Slowly, we realize that the Lomax sisters

have created an idiosyncratic world of juxtaposed images, chosen as much for their aesthetic and (we suppose) symbolic nature, as for their geographic appropriateness.

The Lomax quilt's composition seems to owe something to twentieth-century painting. With its intuitively balanced palette and small, precise shapes it looks great as a whole—rather like a Cubist composition—even if it is a bit awkward to "read" as a travelogue. Many blocks face left, but then suddenly some face forward. In some blocks we look in vain for images, but find only bits of patchwork; in others the pieces of fabric form very specific pictures of people and places, animals and pots of flowers. We glimpse tableaux of Mexico, New England, India, and Egypt. We see some unexpected images like the carefully embroidered royal carriage in the lower right and the mushrooms near the top right. The black frame and the large areas of black in the center are echoed throughout the quilt, pulling the composition together visually.

The aesthetic is modern but there are few images rooting the quilt in the decade of its creation. Time has stopped. In this land of counterpane it could be 1880 or 1960. In fact, the world was at war and life was uncertain when the Lomax sisters sat down with their needles. They must have found comfort in their work as a new world took shape beneath their skillful fingers. ✩

THE
"COLOR GARDEN" QUILT

JANE SASSAMAN DOESN'T WANT much. She only wants to dazzle her viewers. "I want to snap them out of a mundane routine and remind them that they are part of a bigger cosmic picture," says the Chicago quilt artist. "I want to express the energy and mystery of our amazing universe." While this may be a universal artistic wish, Sassaman has an unusually good head start on the project. Each of her quilts is a memorable view of the Garden of Eden, teeming with color and shape, plunging us into jungles of fronds, gardens of blossoms. In these tactile chronicles of nature-run-wild we cannot help but sense the raw energy the artist pours into her work—an effort that always leaves her exhausted but happy at completion. "When a large quilt is finished I am totally burnt out and doubting if I'll ever make another one," she says. "But after a week or so . . . I begin to get those idea sparks and off I go again."

Those sparks (also described by Sassaman as "inklings" and "flashes") are pictorial images that come to her and get her started on her fabric odysseys. After putting down in pencil a rough sketch of the idea in her mind's eye, the next stage is all about shapes. Sassaman collects them, keeping a sketchbook of odd ones, and amassing a

large, flat box of fabric pieces to be kept at hand and dipped into, like dabs of paint on a palette. Both positives and negatives of fabric squiggles, swirls, etc., cut out by Sassaman for this or some previous project, go into this box and then out again, as fishing around, Sassaman alights upon one or the other and adds it to her current mix taking shape on the wall in front of her. "I get a group of shapes that intrigue me and I put it here, I try it there," she says. "It's all about what I call "squinting time." I sometimes feel a little ridiculous during this period. After studying various arrangements all day, I find myself sneaking up on the piece to get a fresh perspective."

Finally the shapes and colors have coalesced into another view of paradise. Sassaman begins the process of keeping them there, and adding to their effectiveness by what she describes as "painting with thread." "I shade and sculpt individual pieces, zigzagging dark thread on one edge and light on the other. It's a way to add highlights with thread." The fabric pieces themselves are mostly cotton, and are first held to the background with masking tape, and then machine-appliquéd, sometimes one over another, to achieve a tangled overgrown collage effect. The completed quilt top is then attached to layers of batting and backing and machine-quilted, providing another layer of decorative clout.

At 43 x 43 inches, Color Garden by Jane Sassaman is a versatile splash of color guaranteed to draw the eye— a reminder of the endless fascination of nature.

Although thoroughly modern in her aesthetic, Sassaman sees many parallels between her work and that of quilters of previous generations. Like those before her who chose patterns like Grandma's Flower Garden and

Sunshine and Shadow, she has chosen the beauty of the world as her subject. Also like her ancestors, she is frugal with her fabric, often using leftover shapes from one quilt in the construction of the next. Among her other influences are all kinds of historic embroideries. "I enjoy my connection with centuries of fiber artists," says Sassaman. "Sure it's 'woman's work.' That's where its power is."

Sassaman herself has been a fiber artist only since 1980. She received a bachelor's degree from Iowa State University where she specialized in textile design and jewelry-making, and then worked as a window dresser, sign maker, illustrator, and designer of decorative accessories. Sassaman also continued to develop fabric-related interests including painting, embroidery, soft sculpture, and costume design. "I was looking for my medium," she remembers. The rightness of quiltmaking, a process she describes as "soft painting," hit her like a thunderbolt. "It satisfies every dimension," says Sassaman. "It has color, craftsmanship, engineering, graphic power, the physical aspect of the textiles. It's like putting together a puzzle too. Quilting has taken over my life. All of my thoughts are now interpreted with fabric and thread. It's my language."

THE
SUNBURST PATTERN
QUILT

THIS PATTERN IS DAZZLING—exploding like a series of celestial events, popping and waning in tight formation across the quilt top. Yet it is also quite elegant —a bird's-eye view of a formal garden in full bloom, a glance at a priceless cache of glass paperweights, each with a kaleidoscopic moment trapped within its transparent sphere. All of this visual delight comes to us courtesy of a complicated, illusionary pattern called Sunburst and a startlingly large selection of nineteenth-century cottons. The result is a work that typifies the best of early American quiltmaking.

Star patterns of all sorts were typical of the first half of the last century—confluences of triangles coming together at various angles—an entire firmament of shining symbols representing their makers' interest in the heavens and the new republic. When quilters added an outer ring of trianglar points to basic star shapes like the LeMoyne or Lone Star, they created a whole new genre of patterns known as the Starburst or Blazing Star. With the substitution of a central circle, such patterns left the star category entirely, bursting out on their own to become Sunburst, Blazing Sun, Sunflower, or Mariner's Compass—depending on the size of the center and the disposition of the surrounding points.

All of these sunny-starry explosions were slightly different, but they meant the same thing for the prospective quilter: She had to know exactly what she was doing. Every one of her tiny triangles had to fit perfectly against the next or the entire pattern, not to mention the quilt, would pucker and pull dreadfully. When the work was done properly, however, the result was considered such a masterpiece that the quilt was not used, instead it was kept "for best" and passed down from generation to generation. Makers lavished their finest quilting on these carefully pieced examples, filling the expanses between the pieced areas with exquisite quilted and stuffed designs.

Our maker, working around 1840, seemed to have quite another agenda. This example is not quilted at all. Although that may be because she simply never got around to it, a more likely explanation was her complete preoccupation with the possibilities of the Sunburst pattern itself. Between the seventy-two different sunburst variations crowded in here, there's barely room for a single quilted twining vine. Our maker has dispensed with every other kind of ornament—there are no borders for example—and she hasn't allowed herself the graphic clout of allover patterning, allowing half-sunbursts at the edges to continue the pattern into infinity. Every sunburst is whole and complete because this quilt is really a showcase for a single proposition: The same Sunburst pieced pattern will look completely different depending on how and where the varying fabrics are placed.

The colorful pieced circles of the Sunburst pattern echo the shape of this table top, while the unquilted quilt "top" makes a smooth, unbulky covering.

There are at least seventy-five different fabrics represented here—a true cross section of the huge selection available to the public a full twenty-five years before the

Civil War. In the world of calicoes, it was a heady era. American mills were producing over 120 million yards every year and, particularly on the East Coast, dry goods shops were a festival of color and pattern. Roller printing, then a relatively new technology, was producing many novel special effects, including "cracked ice" and other finely printed backgrounds, and crisp, small-scale patterning. There were cheery pinks and warm browns along with plenty of reds, yellows, and blues—all seen here in profusion.

Our quilter had a field day with all of this bounty, playing with the relationships between dark and light, larger and smaller patterns, carefully employing the occasional solid to vary the mix. By juxtaposing certain fabrics, she effectively emphasized and deemphasized parts of the Sunburst pattern, making it appear that there are more, then fewer, "rings" of triangles, or that the shapes are slightly bigger or smaller. No two sunbursts are alike. Some look more like flowers, others more like true stars. We blink and look again, and realize that every sunburst is put together exactly the same way. It is a tour de force of fabric selection and placement. It's the quiltmaker's art in action. ✩

THE
"BREAK
THE
SILENCE"
QUILT

WHENEVER BONNIE PETERSON exhibits her quilt *Break the Silence,* she places a sign nearby that reads: PLEASE TOUCH. Coming from an artist, this may seem a strange exhortation, but Peterson is hoping her viewers will get up close and personal with her work—stroke it, examine it carefully back and front—and in so doing, discover its secrets. For in *Break the Silence* every one of the warm, friendly-looking houses hides an unpleasant truth—the existence of domestic violence. Viewers need only flip up any one of these cheery symbols of familial contentment—each of which remains attached by its roof —to find poignant messages and quotations on the subject lurking underneath, ("do what I say or I'll be angry, you just can't take a joke, tell someone"). "Domestic violence occurs in houses of all sizes, at every income level," says Peterson. "I'm just reminding people that what looks beautiful on the outside may be very different inside."

Break the Silence *by Bonnie Peterson becomes an interactive work of art when viewers lift up charming appliquéd houses to reveal messages about domestic violence.*

Peterson has tackled many such political and social issues in her quilts—from breast cancer to bovine growth hormones. Preachy impersonality, however, is hardly her

tell someone

inequality
competition
hostility
control
negation
explosion
denial
threats

manipulation

style. "I try to express with fabric the concepts, ideas, and dreams in my life." she says. "I use the creative process to work out questions, frustrations, and goals." In a work Peterson has dubbed her *Bra Quilt* for example, she uses humor to attract her audience—dotting her quilt with facsimiles of brassieres—getting viewers laughing, but also discussing their fears of breast cancer. *Break the Silence* is quite purposefully a friendly, folksy kind of piece—Grandma Moses meets Robert Rauschenberg—with dangling, glittering add-ons and seductive, velvety fabrics. Surely nothing bad can happen in this colorful evocation of the all-American home and hearth. Think again.

Not surprisingly, Peterson's background is somewhat unusual for a quiltmaker. "I was going to be a shrink," she laughs, remembering. "I studied psychology and sociology, and also completed my MBA. For a while I worked as a marketing researcher for a chemical company." Taking up traditional quiltmaking as a hobby in 1985, Peterson immediately became bored cutting and piecing strips and began to make small, nontraditional fabric wall hangings. A friend's death from cancer was the catalyst for a nontraditional quilt made "as therapy," and shortly thereafter, a grant from the Illinois Arts Council convinced her that as a budding professional quiltmaker she "was on the right track." Since then Peterson has exhibited and sold quilts dealing with her many personal interests, including backpacking and the outdoors, as well as social and political issues like that of *Break the Silence*.

Along with its important message, this particular quilt was born out of a longtime wish of Peterson's: "I always wanted to make a Crazy Quilt," she admits. Working on a wall, on a single prepared fabric surface, she appliquéd various dark, irregularly shaped velvet pieces—fifteen different houses and attached surroundings—to her background. She rubber stamped the messages inside the houses (the edges of which were burned)—and photo-transferred the images of the actual houses that accompany the messages. Just as in a Crazy Quilt, the top surface was then embellished with every kind of shiny, attractive, decorative touch: Over fifty kinds of wool, rayon, metallic yarn, glass, and metal were used. Keys and charms hang from the houses. The yarn was knotted and hung like tassels, and then embellished with glass beads. Along with a number of sad, "broken" houses, these hang from the piece itself, visible from front or back. Written in fabric on the back of the quilt is the message BREAK THE SILENCE AT YOUR HOUSE.

It's a message Peterson hopes will be read, and understood, viscerally, through her preferred medium. "The quilt medium is tactile, it's accessible, it's not intimidating," she points out. "I like to watch people lifting up these houses and reading the messages. It always gets them talking about their own experiences, and that's what we need." ☆

THE "ON DWIGHT WAY" QUILT

SOMETIMES BEAUTIFUL THINGS are just meant to be. This one came about because of a fortuitous confluence of impressions made on an artist in the right place at the right time. Modesto, California quiltmaker Yvonne Porcella had been to a Monet exhibition in San Francisco where she had been particularly struck by the sight of a late painting of wisteria, executed when the aging Impressionist was nearly blind. Shortly afterward, while visiting her daughter in Berkeley on a street called Dwight Way, the sight of a nearby pergola dripping with heavy wisteria blossoms recalled to Porcella the power of Monet's nearly abstract flowers. She too wanted to record the beauty of the wisteria and the almost palpable feeling of spring she had just experienced.

Yvonne Porcella was in a perfect position to do so for she was, and is, one of the best known fabric artists in the country. Her career began back in the 1960s when she began to weave cloth on her loom and then make clothing to sell out of it. In the 1970s, she switched to the creation of patchwork wearable art, and by 1981, she was incorporating her unique textiles into art quilts. Porcella had found her niche and one year later gave up her day job (in nursing) to devote herself to a new and stellar career. In 1997 she was inducted into the selective Quilters Hall of Fame and one of her quilts was exhibited, in the company of works by Rodin and Picasso, in the exhibition commemorating the 150th birthday of the Smithsonian Institution in Washington, D.C.

"Marble fudge ice cream, slightly melted and

stirred—that's the color and pattern I wanted and it became the reason I began to experiment with textile paints," Porcella wrote in her 1997 book *Six Color World.* Change the flavor to butterscotch with a little grape on the side and the same evocative image applies to the background fabrics used in *On Dwight Way.* To make this quilt, Porcella began with various white silks—including pongee, silk twill, and organza—and painted them with textile paint thinned with water (to prevent buildup that would clog the silk) in "colors that harmonize." To create spontaneous allover patterns, dictated by the serendipitous way each fabric absorbed the color—much like the technique used to create marbled paper.

Choosing a single piece of this colored fabric as her background, she overpainted her composition, defining some of its shapes. Pieces of the purple and green fabrics destined to become part of Porcella's wisteria were then burned at the edges until they attained the proper shape. The charred bits were rubbed off and the leaves and petals laid onto

Quilt artist Yvonne Porcella's fascination with things Japanese is obvious in her lyrical depiction of wisteria vines at the height of their bloom.

the background and appliquéd, without turning under the edges. Batting and backing were added and the composition was quilted in an abstract geometric pattern completely different from the twining, naturalistic blossoms, while silk ribbon was used to form the wisteria vine. The final composition is neither painted nor applied, but a subtle combination of both. The hand-painted fabric itself, Porcella's overpaint, and the pieces of burnt silk appliqué juxtapose each other, adding layers of color and shape, and creating an impression of sun and blossoms that becomes difficult (and pointless) to deconstruct.

Porcella recalls that when the quilt was finished it seemed too small. By flanking the central compostion with narrow panels of hand-painted lavender silk, Porcella added needed inches and also brought the quilt into the realm of the Oriental screen, already evoked by an asymmetrical placement of blossoms and the empty space that balances her composition in the Japanese way. In fact, Porcella is interested in all things Japanese. Her fascination with Asian art began twenty-five years ago with a chance reading of *The Tale of Genji,* a tenth-century novel by an unknown woman of the court, replete with descriptions of kimonos in sensuous colors, and has continued through two recent trips to Japan.

Like the maker of a Japanese screen, Porcella has created a subtle, textured background and then suggested an entire realm of sun and flowers with a few well-placed shapes. The screen maker stretches the painted paper or fabric in a wooden frame for strength; Porcella backs and quilts her work for the same reason. Both objects have traditional, practical uses that do not include a position on the wall, but this does not dilute our enjoyment of their beauty when we put them there. Looking at *On Dwight Way,* we cannot imagine how any other medium could so eloquently convey an artist's experience of heavy, hanging blossoms and sun-filled air.

THE
PARADISE
GARDEN
QUILT

THIS FABULOUS QUILT is an example of the power of the press—and of one book in particular. It was 1929 when author Ruth Findlay wrote *Old Patchwork Quilts and the Women Who Made Them*. Throughout the 1920s there was a nationwide revival of all things Colonial. Naturally women became interested in quilting again. Their goal was to decorate their new suburban Colonial bedrooms with simple American four-posters and traditional American bedcovers that looked as though they could have been made in Salem, Massachusetts, in about 1820. Ms. Findlay fanned the flames of the new enthusiasm for American quilting by writing about classic patterns and the quilters who had used them.

On one page of her popular book she featured a medallion-style appliqué quilt from 1857 made by Arsinoe Kelsey Bowen of Cortland, New York, which Bowen had called a Garden Quilt. Findlay praised the quilt heartily, calling it "the acme of the branch of the art" (presumably referring to the art of detailed appliqué). Before long copies of the 5-inch-square photo that appeared in the book were blown up and drafted into free, usable quilt patterns that spread like wildfire, hand to hand, among the nation's quilters. Suddenly everybody wanted to make a Garden Quilt. Demand was so great that even during the straitened 1930s, an official, printed, hand-colored Garden Quilt pattern cost a whopping $5.

The pattern became a favorite with competitive quilters and apparently with quilt judges who saw the complicated floral design as a natural showcase for virtuoso appliqué, quilting, and embroidery techniques. The Garden phenomenon stretched nationwide and lasted for decades. In 1933 a Mrs. Emma Craig of Emporia, Kansas, won the Kansas State Fair quilt competition with a Garden Quilt, while a Mrs. Florence Lourette of Rochester, New York, took home a third prize medal from the 1940 New York World's Fair with her version. Not to be outdone, the famous quilt designer Rose Kretsinger, (1886–1963) came out of semi-retirement and produced a quilt she called Paradise Garden. With this masterpiece she won a

A favorite with competitive quilters of the 1930s and 40s, the Paradise Garden pattern produced elaborate, elegant quilts like this one.

series of prizes at Kansas fairs in the 1940s and 1950s. In fact, Kretsinger's version became so well known and came to occupy such an important place in her life's work that she singled it out for a great personal honor. Lying ill in a hospital late in life, Kretsinger asked that all of her quilts be laid flat on the bed next to her. On top, draped over all, was her Paradise Garden—positioned so that she could reach over and touch it.

We know little about Arsinoe Kelsey Bowen, the woman who started it all (except that her grandniece was a neighbor of Ruth Findlay's), and just as little about A. Y., the Cape Cod woman who made this version in 1935. We do know that A. Y. was an expert quilter with a great sense of style. With twelve to fourteen stitches per inch, her quilt is a symphony of miniaturized detail. She used a plethora of techniques—appliqué, embroidery, overlapping fabric, and elaborate quilting—to create an almost three-dimensional tribute to nature. The colorful appliqué grabs our attention first, but upon closer inspection we realize that this masterpiece owes its depth to the fine, complicated floral quilting all around the appliqué.

Every bird, every berry, every flower is represented in realistic detail but none take away from the pleasing, overall composition. There is nothing overly studied about A. Y.'s central ring of American birds—even if the plumage is recorded in surprising and correct detail. Although the central medallion style she employs was typical of the eighteenth century, the quilt is not a pseudo-eighteenth-century quilt but rather a twentieth-century version of a classic style. The palette is clearly influenced by the 1930s preference for cheery pastels, and there is an echo of the floral effusions of early-twentieth-century designers like Marie Webster in the design. Above all the quilt creates a feeling of lushness, of the never-ending bounty of nature, an effect that must have been very comforting at the height of the Depression. For many days and nights during the difficult 1930s, this quilter took her needle in hand and escaped to paradise. ☆

SILK
CHERRY
TREE
QUILT

IS THIS A LONG-LOST EXAMPLE by one of Kentucky's most famous quilters? She was Virginia Mason Ivey of Logan County, Kentucky, the daughter of a notable local family. Her father, Captain David Ivey, had fought with Andrew Jackson at the battle of New Orleans in 1812. Virginia was his second daughter, named for the Captain's home state, and as she remained unmarried, spent her life devoted to her father and other relatives and in the cultivation of fine needlework. Her quilts were soon famous, collecting prize after prize at state and local fairs.

In 1856 Virginia outdid herself, producing a fabulous white quilt now in the collection of the Smithsonian Institution in Washington, D.C. It is entitled "A Representation of the Fairground Near Russellville, Kentucky," and is a masterpiece of stitchery, depicting a ring and exhibition tent surrounded by horseback riders, carriages, fair visitors, and livestock, all surrounded by trees. The stuffed work or trapunto areas of the design are actually three-dimensional, having been stuffed with batting or string. Every detail, from the horses' harnasses to the spokes in the carriage wheels, are clearly visible. This quilt is one of the most famous ever to come out of Kentucky, so experts have long had their eyes out for other examples.

It was not until the mid-1980s that a second Ivey quilt surfaced. Executed ca. 1850 or some six years before her more representational masterpiece, this quilt appears to be more conventionally floral, with vines, fruit trees, and the odd bird added for color. But a closer look at its white stuffed work reveals a depiction of a statue of Henry Clay and a man on horseback thought to be Andrew Jackson—her father's old companion in arms. Stuffed-work animals surrounding these two gentlemen include horses, dogs, birds, ducks, cows, and pigs. As in the Smithsonian's Fairground quilt, the detailing is astounding. A prime example by a Kentucky quilter, this masterpiece soon found a home at Louisville's Speed Art Museum.

Now we get to the mystery: The family of Virginia Ivey has always reported the existence of at least one other wonderful quilt. It has been described as being made of silk—possibly black silk. Could the quilt in this picture be Virginia Ivey's lost masterpiece? We know that this quilt came from a Kentucky family and that it dates back around 1850. This one isn't black, but it is silk with black edging, and there are a number of similarities among it and the other quilts known to have been crafted by Ivey. Next there are the intriguing stylistic similarities: The Speed Art Museum's quilt boasts an unusual wavy border of colored stuffed work surrounded with distinctive featherlike quilting, over which flowering vines alternate with grape vines, just inside and outside of its permineter. This quilt has the same, distinctive border.

Next, there is the matter of the cherry trees: In the Speed quilt, such trees are placed obliquely to the center medallion and alternate with those of other species. In our quilt cherry trees are the main event, spaced evenly across the quilt, growing right side up, whichever way you turn it. Cherry trees are not a particularly common motif to begin with, and these are the very same four-branched little trees found in the Speed quilt, heavy with cherries and featuring the same spreading, rakelike bottom. The quilting, set into triangular pieces between the trees, is of a different pattern than that of Ivey's other known quilts, but is every bit as complex and finely worked.

Of course it is entirely possible that some skilled quilter of Miss Ivey's acquaintance, having admired her neighbor's wonderful quilts at any number of state fairs, finally took it upon herself to co-opt her unusual style. This copyist may have borrowed some motifs and not others—there are no animals or birds in this quilt, for example—and created a very similar quilt. Then again, this could be the real thing—an Ivey quilt. Could a scientist in some laboratory measure the stitches or examine the thread content used to make each quilt and come up with a definitive answer about who made this example? Probably. But that wouldn't be any fun. Far better to compare and wonder, look and ponder among the cherry trees. ✿

Although Crazy Quilts were often made of silks and satins, early silk quilts with appliqué and stuffed work (trapunto) like this 1850s example are rare.

THE
BRODERIE
PERSE
QUILT

AS THE CIVIL WAR RAGED around them, the inhabitants of Charleston and Savannah must have wondered if their elegant, well-mannered world was coming to an end. Tucked away among their shady streets, at least one of their number was determined to retain something of the Old World while embracing the new. Jane Gatchel was one of the lucky Southerners who possessed, in spite of blockades and hard times, a sufficient supply of cloth to continue what must have been a stellar quilting career. Between 1861 and 1865, she created this unusual Broderie Perse quilt—a perfect blending of the delicate floral appliqué so dear to the prewar South and the bright colors and strong graphics of the "modern" quilt.

By 1861 the plantations near Charleston had long been known as producers of Broderie Perse—although they probably called it by another name. It wasn't until late in the nineteenth century that the term, which translates to Persian Embroidery, came into common usage. Also known as Cretonne Appliqué and Cut-Out Chintz Appliqué, the practice involved the careful cutting out of chintz elements like birds and floral sprays and appliquéing them onto a new ground in a pleasing pattern. It was the fabric equivalent of decoupage and had much to recommend it, as it made a small amount of expensive chintz go a long, long way. It also freed the quilter to be creative—to combine different elements, for example, adding a bird or a few butterflies to a flowering branch, or to put two different sprays of flowers together to produce something new and beautiful.

The origins of chintz appliqué are rather uncertain. Some believe it was first practiced in seventeenth-century Europe, others insist that it was actually a homegrown American idea. However it got to our shores, by 1800 a newly fledged America had embraced it so eagerly that some American textile mills were printing fabric actually designed to be cut up and used in this way. As to its exotic moniker, the term may have been coined in 1851 at the Crystal Palace Exhibition in London. There everything "eastern" was deemed fashionable, especially if it had a French name. On the other hand, "Persian" may actually be an uninformed reference to India, from where the chintz fabric came.

Whatever its name, the practice of chintz appliqué went through several stages. Early-nineteenth-century quilters tended to arrange their elements in the then-fashionable, central medallion style. By 1840, in the wake of the fad for album quilts, a block style of arrangement became more common. Even later, fabric cutouts were used as much for their color as for their design, but Broderie Perse quilts of any kind made after 1865 are rare. Post-Civil War tariffs made imported chintz an unaffordable luxury for many, and American chintz was never as popular. Perhaps because of this, furnishing with chintz went out of style, and with it the Broderie Perse quilt. Calico, the backbone of the American textile industry, became the fabric of choice for late-nineteenth-century-quilters.

Fortunately, many beautiful Broderie Perse quilts still survive. Too elaborate to use as bedcovers, they were often made as a presentation object—presented as a gift on an important occasion—or for a best quilt, to be used only when important visitors were in the house. Such quilts were put carefully away and suffered no hard wear. Mrs. Gatchel's quilt is in beautiful condition, allowing us to enjoy all forty-eight of her different appliqué elements. There seems to be no end to her ingenuity in combining birds, insects, flowers, baskets, and ribbons, some of which are positioned at different angles to vary their decorative punch. Perhaps as a nod to the past, she couldn't resist including a large central element of appliqué, yet she also emphasized the modern block format by adding small elements in the corner blocks between squares. Her bright red sashing increases the graphic power of this quilt beyond that of the usual album. The sashing and the red, white, and green zig-zag borders beyond them are clearly not there just to present the floral elements they enclose. They are part of an overall decorative pattern characteristic of many late-nineteenth-century American quilts. In 1865 much of the South was struggling to enter the modern era, but not Mrs. Gatchel. She was already there. ✩

With its appliquéd elements of floral chintz (Broderie Perse), crimson sashing, and zig-zag borders, this quilt exudes Southern charm.

A M I S H
DOUBLE
WEDDING
RING
Q U I L T

MIDWESTERN AMISH QUILTS combine the best of all possible worlds. Amish quilters living in the nation's heartland in the 1930s and 1940s took their special blend of virtuoso quilting and superb color sense and applied it to a wide repertoire of the most beloved, popular American patterns. While the Lancaster Amish confined themselves largely to simple medallion and bar forms —deeming them more "modest" and "humble" than fashionable mainstream patterns—Midwestern Amish communities allowed quilters much more freedom. Their quilters took the most beautiful patterns their "English" neighbors had to offer and made them their own. The results were often spectacular—as in this Double Wedding Ring quilt, made in Ohio in about 1940.

East and Central Ohio boast the largest concentrations of Amish people in the world. Their forebears came to Holmes and Tuscarawas Counties in the early nineteenth century—part of a general migration westward in search of new farmland. They formed stable, economically prosperous communities in which women were both well trained in needlework and had sufficient time for quilting. Many also had the church "permission" that their Lancaster sisters lacked. Although like all Amish people they valued modesty, community, and hard work and eschewed many worldly vanities, some of the Ohio communities were influenced by the comparative liberality of the Mennonite and other communities with whom they lived side by side for many decades.

Midwestern Amish behavior was (and is) governed by individual church groups, so that one Amish family might have lived quite differently than the one just across the road. Some communities permitted almost any kind of quilt to be made; others proscribed patterns and colors. If a quilter married into a stricter church group, she may have had to put away some of her quilts and become careful about future production. Patterns and colors also varied from community to community and from state to state, as a matter of tradition and taste. Brown cloth, for example, was favored by the Nebraska Amish but eschewed by most Pennsylvanians.

Ohio Amish quilts were made in almost every hue and are reknowned for their wide variety of complex and original patterns—everything from Tumbling Blocks to Ocean Waves. For many Amish makers, these patterns seemed natural outgrowths of what they saw around them in daily life—furrows, barn rafters, buggy wheels, the stars in the sky. Quilts were executed most frequently in cotton—not wool like those in Lancaster County. Between 1920 and 1940 black became a favorite background color; it is the Amish color of joy and an excellent foil for the striking visual designs Midwestern quiltmakers favored.

The Double Wedding Ring pattern was an extremely popular choice among all early-twentieth-century American quilters. Among the Amish however, there was a certain irony about this pattern's popularity: Amish rules of dress forbade the wearing of all jewelry—even wedding rings.

Amish quilters probably saw Double Wedding Ring simply as an opportunity for intricate color play. The maker of this quilt has used a subtle palette of unusual, contrasting colors, presented in small, precise pieces, to form the rings of the pattern. No ring is exactly the same as any other, but the balance of color in the quilt as a whole is perfect. Interspersions of black anchor the rings to the background and heighten the illusionary aspect of the pattern. As we view it, we begin to ask ourselves—which ring is on top of which?

Our Ohio quilter probably had to work up to Double Wedding Ring; round shapes are difficult to sew and the scalloped border raises the ante even further. Somebody obviously wanted to preserve the final effect—this quilt has never been washed. Makers reveled in the fact that the edges of their masterpieces would never be tucked under a mattress, adding many decorative flourishes to finish them. In this example,

This setting points up the timeless, classic nature of many American quilt patterns. This example of the Double Wedding Ring quilt was executed against a black background—the Amish color of joy.

silk, velvet, and lace have been combined to form a charming border that emphasizes the fragile materials and rich color scheme of the quilt. Oscar Wilde's sunflower is front and center, as are other traditional Crazy motifs like fans and birds. Because of its construction, a Crazy was naturally organized into squares, but in this one those squares form no unifying design. Each square is an individual composition; the whole is balanced only by the strategic placement of Japanese-influenced fans. The maker has provided many embroidered motifs to anchor the design but has not overwhelmed her creation with cobwebby white stitching.

With all its flowers, lace, and fans, this is a rather feminine quilt that would not have been out of place in a Victorian boudoir. In fact, it is just the perfect size to drape over a satin chaise longue. Missing are the more masculine elements—commemorative ribbons from military campaigns or horse shows and the other symbols of family history that many Crazy Quilts feature. This example seems less about memory than about beauty, richness, and charm. ✩

THE SAMPLER QUILT

MENTION THE WORDS "sampler quilt" and your listener will probably picture a yellowing expanse of quilted linen embroidered with optimistic homilies and cross-stitched alphabets. In actuality, a sampler quilt is more like a Whitman's Sampler than the embroidered samplers that hang on the wall. It is a block-style quilt designed to acquaint the viewer with all of the delicious patterns the quilter has to offer, those from quilts she has already made and those she hopes to make. Such a quilt is a file drawer, not a composition, so star patterns abut geometrics and appliquéd blocks crowd triangular piecework with no rhyme or reason. Yet somehow it all works together.

Many sampler quilts were made between 1860 and 1890. Like their sister genre the album quilt, some samplers were a group effort, a quilt constructed by a number of people to be presented to a teacher, needle-work instructor, or other esteemed figure. In such a case each block was signed so the recipient would know who had contributed it. A quilt of unsigned blocks signals a single maker. Both kinds of samplers can be an excellent overview of the quilting tastes of the period. Some quilts, like this one, combined piecework and appliqué. Many contained allover patterns as well as those naturally fit the block format. Some blocks were much larger than others, as if the quilter wanted to say to the world, "Look at this pattern. This was my favorite."

Sampler quilts can be a fascinating road map of the quilter's personality and predilections. About this example we know only that it was made in Ohio in about 1870, but a close look fuels interesting speculation. We can probably rule out the quilter-showing-off theory for this maker has taken the easy way out, using positives and negatives of one pattern, and repeating another pattern in two colorways. She's even thrown in a couple of blocks of printed fabric to fill gaps. Yet there's a definite aesthetic at work here, a preponderance of crosses and Xs—it's almost as if she challenged herself to see how many different variations she could fashion. Perhaps there's a reason for all those straight lines; she doesn't seem to do as well with circular shapes. Some represented here are downright lopsided. The colors in this quilt are so limited that we probably are not dealing with a quilt of leftover blocks, but a record of patterns our maker preferred, all executed at one time, in the fabrics she happened to have at hand.

Those fabrics aren't fancy, so she probably lived in the country. Two patches are in the random style known as crazy patchwork. In their stark abstraction these blocks look a bit incongruous among all the stars and crosses. Although there has been some attempt at strategic placement—three appliqué blocks form a sort of center focus—the maker seems to have been indifferent to the balance of color. Two pink blocks sit together at the top, where most of the quilt's red is also bunched up. She is apparently more interested in shapes; the few circles are spread around nicely, relieving the visual monotony of all those crosses and other straight lines.

And in the end she triumphs. There is a sense of adventure, of individualism, that carries this quilt along and wins our hearts. The quilter has trusted herself and the innate decorative power of the sampler format: Just as almost any group of quilts looks marvelous together, the quilts-in-miniature of the sampler somehow always come together to create a piece of good design. Yet another example of the magic of the American quilt. ✩

So successful is this quilt's design that we have to look closely to realize it is a sampler—a potpourri of one maker's entire repertoire of patterns.

QUILT
CARE

ANTIQUE QUILTS can be a fragile commodity. To preserve them for yourself and for the next generation, here are a few simple ideas.

CLEANING

CLEAN ANTIQUE QUILTS as infrequently as possible, only when it is unavoidable. Wool or silk quilts will fare best if they are taken to a professional dry cleaner who specializes in antique textiles (not your general-service corner dry cleaner). Cotton or linen quilts may be washed at home but first need to be tested for colorfastness. Apply a few drops of water in an inconspicuous place, blot with a white blotter (a scrap of clean, white, cotton fabric will do), and check to see if any color comes off on the blotter. If you see any at all, check with your professional dry cleaner. If not, repeat the test with a mild detergent solution.

When you are sure your dyes will not run, you may soak your quilt in a bathtub full of warm water and mild soap, pumping gently up and down and avoiding all unnecessary agitation. Never scrub, squeeze or run water directly on the quilt. Rinse with clear water, repeating as many times as necessary until all the soap is gone. Carefully remove the quilt from the tub, making sure the weight of the wet quilt does not strain the fabric. Squeeze out as much moisture as possible into absorbent towels (never, ever use paper towels), and then lay the quilt, as flat as possible, on more clean towels and leave it to dry out of direct sunlight. Never iron your quilt.

Some experts believe it is preferable to vacuum a quilt. To do so safely, cover it with a fiberglass-coated window screen and then gently vacuum the quilt back and front. The screen will keep the vacuum from sucking in the quilt and damaging it.

Stains are very tricky and are best tackled by a professional. If you want to have a go at it yourself, experts suggest moistening a cotton ball with a 3 percent solution of hydrogen peroxide and applying it to the stain while exposing it to direct sunlight. Add more solution, keeping the area damp, until the stain is removed. This may take several hours. Rinse well. Remember that such exposure to sunlight may fade colored areas of the quilt.

STORAGE

WRAP YOUR QUILT loosely in a clean sheet, folding it as few times as possible. Lay it flat with nothing heavy on top. Never store your quilt in a plastic bag or allow it to come into direct contact with a wooden shelf or moth balls. Some experts say its best to avoid mothballs completely. Store your quilts in a clean, dry place. Remove once or twice a year and refold, allowing no permanent creases to form and checking to see that no damage has occurred. Some experts suggest a good airing, out of doors on a dry, clear day. But, of course, avoid direct sunlight.

MISCELLANEOUS

WHEN HANDLING VERY OLD, fragile quilts, it's best to wear cotton gloves because the oils in your hands can be very damaging. Mending a quilt is another job for an expert, but if you are a good seamstress and want to do the work yourself, remember to hand-sew any repairs you make to a hand sewn quilt and to use only period fabric for patching or replacement. Modern fabric will stand out and look odd. Be on the look out for old, damaged, inexpensive quilts from which salvagable pieces might be cut.

Quilts can be displayed anywhere and are meant to be enjoyed, but if you plan to hang your quilt, remember that years of direct sunlight will damage it. Also, try to keep windows closed (to prevent blowing dirt from damaging fibers) in the room where it is displayed and consider running an air conditioner in that room year-round to keep the temperature and humidity constant. Humidity should be kept at approximately 50 percent and the temperature should remain on the cool side. One last caveat: When hanging a quilt to display its charms, consider using a stretcher with Velcro on all four sides (less damaging to fibers) or folding the quilt over a padded, muslin-covered dowel. Both look nice and will not damage the quilt.

QUILT RESOURCES

The following is a selective list of museums, galleries, and dealers that offers sources for viewing and purchasing both antique and contemporary quilts. In each case, it is a good idea to call in advance to make sure the quilts you are interested in are currently on display or available.

ALABAMA

Birmingham Museum
of Art
2000 8th Avenue North
Birmingham, AL 35203
(205) 254-2966

Robert Cargo
Folk Art Gallery
2314 Sixth Street
Tuscaloosa, AL 35401
(205) 758-8884

ARIZONA

The Quilted Apple
3043 N. 24th Street
Phoenix, AZ 85016
(602) 956-0904
Laurene Sinema

CALIFORNIA

American Museum of
Quilts & Textiles
60 South Market Street
San Jose, CA 95112
(408) 971-0323

The Ames Gallery
of American Folk Art
2661 Cedar Street
Berkeley, CA 94708
(510) 845-4949
Bonnie Grossman

Calico Antiques
611 North Alta Drive
Beverly Hills, CA 90210
(310) 273-4192

East Meets West Antiques
160 North LaBrea Avenue
Los Angeles, CA 90036
(213) 931-0500

Judith Litvich
Contemporary Fine Art
#2 Henry Adams
San Francisco, CA 94103
(415) 863-3329

Penny Nii Quilt Art
1017 Cathcart Way
Stanford, CA
www.penny-nii.com
(415) 493-5618

The Quilt Gallery
1015 Montana Avenue
Santa Monica, CA 90403
(310) 393-1148
Ludie Strauss

Quilt San Diego/VISIONS
1205 J Street Suite A
San Diego, CA 92101
(619) 702-2020

Sandy White Antique Quilts
105 W. Chapman Avenue
Orange, CA 92866
(714) 639-3424 or
(818) 988-0575

DELAWARE

Winterthur Museum,
Garden & Library
The Henry Francis du Pont
Winterthur Museum
Winterthur, DE 19735
(302) 888-4600

GEORGIA

Connell Gallery
333 Buckhead Avenue
Atlanta, GA 30305
(404) 261-1712
Martha Connell

ILLINOIS

Illinois State Museum
Spring and Edwards Streets
Springfield, IL 62706
(217) 782-7152

INDIANA

Indianapolis Museum of Art
1200 West 38th Street
Indianapolis, IN 46208-4196
(317) 923-1331

KANSAS

Spencer Museum of Art
The Univeristy of Kansas
Lawrence, Kansas 66045
(913) 864-4710

KENTUCKY

Museum of American
Quilter's Society
P.O. Box 1540
Paducah, KY 42002-1540
(502) 442-8856

Kentucky Historical Society
Corner of Broadway
and Lewis
P.O. Box H
Frankfort, KY 40601
(502) 564-3016

The Kentucky Museum
Western Kentucky
University
One Big Red Way
Bowling Green, KY
42101-3576
(502) 745-2592

Quilts, etc.
12-z River Hill Road
Louisville, KY 40207
(502) 897-7566
zegartquilt@aol.com
Shelly Zegart

LOUISIANA

The Quilt Cottage
801 Nashville Avenue
New Orleans, LA 70115
(504) 895-3791
Georgia Trist

MAINE

The Marston House
Route 1 at Middle Street
Wicasset, ME 04578
(207) 882-6010

MARYLAND

all of us americans folk art
P.O. Box 30440
Bethesda, MD 20824
(301) 652-4626
Bettie Mintz

Cathy Smith
P.O. Box 681
Severna Park, MD 21146
(301) 647-3503

Stella Rubin Quilts and
   Antiques
12300 Glen Road
Potomac, MD 20854
(301) 958-4187

MASACHUSETTS

Historic Deerfield, Inc.
Box 321
Deerfield, MA 01342
(413) 774-5581

New England Quilt Museum
18 Shattuck Street
Lowell, MA 01852
(978) 452-4207

MICHIGAN

Michigan State University
   Museum at East Lansing
West Circle Dr.
East Lansing, MI 48824
(517) 355-2373

NEBRASKA

International Quilt
   Study Center
HE234
University of Nebraska
   at Lincoln 68583
(402) 472-6301

NEW JERSEY

Americana by the Seashore
604 Broadway
Barnegat Light
Long Beach Island, NJ 08006
(609) 494-0656
Margaret Rapp

NEW MEXICO

Quilts, Ltd.
652 Canyon Road
Santa Fe, NM 87501
(505) 988-5888

NEW YORK

Judi Boisson Antique
American Quilts
96 Main St.
Southampton, NY 11968
(516) 283-5466

Laura Fisher Antiques
1050 Second Avenue
Gallery 84
New York, NY 10022
(212) 838-2596

Metropolitan Museum
   of Art
1000 Fifth Avenue
New York, NY 10028
(212) 879-5500

Museum of American
   Folk Art
Two Lincoln Square
Columbus Avenue between
   65th and 66th Streets
New York, NY 10023
(212) 595-9533

New York State Historical
   Association
Lake Road
Post Office Box 800
Cooperstown, NY 13326
(607) 547-1400

OHIO

Cincinnati Art Museum
Eden Park Drive
Cincinnati, OH 45202
(513) 721-5204

Quilt National
The Dairy Barn Cultural
   Arts Center
8000 Dairy Lane
Post Office Box 747
Athens, OH 45701
(614) 592-4981

OREGON

Cathy Rasmussen
Studio Art Quilt Associates
P.O. Box 287
Dexter, OR 97431

PENNSYLVANIA

Mary & Joe Koval
550 Lutz School Road
Indiana, PA 15701
(412) 465-7370

M. Finkel & Daughter
936 Pine Street
Philadelphia, PA 19107
(215) 627-7797

Vintage Textiles and Tools
P.O. Box 265
Merion, PA 19066
(215) 669-8796
Julie Powell

TENNSESSE

Patchwork Place
340 Main Street
Franklin, TN 37064
(615) 790-1382 or 790-
   8301
Betty Hull

TEXAS

Great Expectations
14520 Memorial Drive,
   Suite 54
Houston, TX 77079
(713) 496-1366
Karey Bresenhan

The International Quilt
   Festival
c/o Quilts, Inc.
7660 Woodway Suite 550
Houston, TX 77063
(713) 781-6864

John Sauls' Antiques
310 West Rusk
P.O. Box 448
Tyler, TX 75710
(214) 593-4668

VERMONT

Marie Miller
Route 30
Dorset, VT 05251
(802) 867-5969

Shelburne Museum
Route 7
Shelburne, VT 05482
(802) 985-3346

VIRGINIA

Abby Aldrich Rockefeller
   Folk Art Center
307 South England Street
Williamsburg, VA 23185
(804) 229-1000

The Valentine Museum
East Clay Street
Richmond, VA 23219
(804) 649-0711

WASHINGTON

The American Art Co.
1126 Broadway Plaza
Tacoma, WA 98402
(800) 753-2278
(253) 272-4327
Rick Gottas

WASHINGTON,
   D.C.

National Museum of
   American History,
   The Smithsonian
Constitution Avenue
   between
   12th and 14th Streets,
   N.W.
Washington, D.C. 20560
(202) 357-1889

CREDITS & ACKNOWLEDGMENTS

We wish to thank the quilt artists and owners who generously lent us quilts for this book:

Karen Felicity Berkenfeld
Joan and Joe Boyle
Laura Fisher
Sue Holdaway-Heys
Sam and Valerie Indenbaum
Barbara Kenworthy
Joan Lintault
Eleanor Bingham Miller
Bonnie Peterson
Yvonne Porcella
Jane A. Sassaman
Robin Schwalb
Kathleen Sharp
Albert and Merry Silber
Harriet and Manny Sklar
Rachel Turner
Miriam Tuska Collection
Herb Wallerstein
John M. Walsh III
Dr. Leslie Williamson
Shelly Zegart

Thanks also to those who graciously allowed the quilts to be photographed in their homes:

Mr. and Mrs. M.L. Berman
Barbara Brody
Laura Lee Brown
Bonnie Caputo
Barbara Darras
Marian DeWitt
Dr. and Mrs. James B. Eckman Jr.
Jenkins Eliason Interiors, Inc
Linda Faiola
Helene Fendelman
Erica Ward and Ralph Gerson
Sam and Valerie Indenbaum
Wayne Jenkins
Kate Johnson
Mr. and Mrs. William Kahn
Louis Keister
Sigrid Christiansen and
    Richard Levey
Julie Rinaldini
Mary Shands
Steve Wilson
Shelly Zegart

Finally, a special thanks to the researchers, stylists, and others who helped make this book possible:

Lori Alpert
Jacqueline M. Atkins
Gayle Benderoff
Lynne Dosker
Deborah Geltman
Ruth Greenstein
Jerry Marshall
Kathy Rasmussen
Terri Zegert Seltz
Christina Sheldon
Julie Silber
Barbara Sturman
Alexandra Truitt
Ron Wolz

PICTURE CREDITS

Pages 35, 39, 45 both, 46 left, 48 both, 49, 50 both, 53 left: CORBIS-BETTMANN
Pages 40, 46 right, 47, 57: The Granger Collection, New York
Pages 41, 54, 61: UPI/CORBIS-BETTMANN
Pages 44, 53 right: Brown Brothers
Page 58: REUTERS/CORBIS-BETTMANN

QUILT LENDER CREDITS

72-75: Laura Fisher/Antique Quilts & Americana; 80, 81, 83: Shelly Zegart; 88, 89: Collection: Albert & Merry Silber; 91: Quilt by Kathleen Sharp © 1997; 92: Quilt by Kathleen Sharp © 1996; 97-99: Collection of Shelly Zegart; 103-105: "The Gift of Tongues" was quilted by Grace Miller, Mt. Joy, PA.; 110, 112, 113: Collection of Albert & Merry Silber; 114, 116, 117: Collection of Herb Wallerstein; 118, 119: Collection of Herb Wallerstein; 121, 122: Collection of Shelly Zegart; 124, 126, 127: Collection of Albert & Merry Silber; 135, 136, 137: Collection of Herb Wallerstein; 138, 139: Collection of John M. Walsh III; 140, 141: Joan Lintault; 142, 143: Collection of Albert & Merry Silber; 152, 154, 155: Laura Fisher/Antique Quilts & Americana; 156, 158, 159: Laura Fisher/Antique Quilts & Americana; 165-167: Rowland and Eleanor Bingham Miller; 175: In the Collection of Mackin and Lynette Smith; 176, 178, 179: Rowland and Eleanor Bingham Miller; 185, 186: Collection of Herb Wallerstein; 188, 190, 191: Collection of Shelly Zegart; 192, 194, 195: Collection of Albert & Merry Silber; 197, 198: Laura Fisher/Antique Quilts & Americana; 209, 210: Bonnie Peterson; 212-214: Yvonne Porcella © 1995 On Dwight Way 34" x 53"; 215-217: Collection of Shelly Zegart; 218, 220: Rowland and Eleanor Bingham Miller; 221-223: Collection of Herb Wallerstein; 228: Rowland and Eleanor Bingham Miller

V

W

Designed by
SUSI OBERHELMAN

The typefaces in this book are
PERPETUA, FUTURA,
and CHANSON D'AMORE

Printed and bound by
TIEN WAH PRESS
SINGAPORE